Developing Effective Teacher Performance

Dr Jeff Jones is Principal Adviser for CfBT (Centre for British Teachers). He has held posts in schools, a Local Education Authority and in Higher Education. He is the author of several books on leadership, management and teacher professional development.

Dr Mazda Jenkin has worked in a number of secondary schools in challenging circumstances. As a head teacher appointed first to a secondary school with serious weaknesses and secondly to one in special measures, she has directly confronted the issues raised in this book, and has studied them further in an Ed.D. at Birmingham University completed in 2004.

Sue Lord is currently a Secondary Strategy Behaviour and Attendance consultant. Her role involves working with senior and middle leaders, classroom teachers and support staff in schools, in developing effective strategies that promote and enhance pupils' learning.

Developing Effective Teacher Performance

Jeff Jones, Mazda Jenkin and Sue Lord

P·C·P

Paul Chapman
Publishing

Paul Chapman Publishing
A SAGE Publications Company
1 Oliver's Yard
55 City Road
London EC1Y 1SP

SAGE Publications Inc.
2455 Teller Road
Thousand Oaks, California 91320

SAGE Publications India Pvt Ltd
B-42, Panchsheel Enclave
Post Box 4109
New Delhi 110 017

Library of Congress Control Number: 2006901380

A catalogue record for this book is available from the
British Library

ISBN-10 1-4129-1928-2   ISBN-13 978-1-4129-1928-9
ISBN-10 1-4129-1929-0   ISBN-13 978-1-4129-1929-6 (pbk)

Typeset by C&M Digitals (P) Ltd., Chennai, India
Printed in Great Britain by Athenaeum Press Ltd., Gateshead, Tyne & Wear
Printed on paper from sustainable resources

Contents

Introduction   vii

1 The challenge to schools posed by
under-performing teachers   1

2 Recognising teacher under-performance   11

3 Supporting teachers to become more effective   26

4 Maintaining teacher performance through self-reflection   45

5 Using performance reviews to develop
teacher performance   75

6 Promoting teacher development – a whole-school
approach to CPD   98

7 Recruiting and selecting effective teachers   116

8 Case-studies: learning through reflection and action   144

Bibliography   159

Index   161

Introduction

Performance will be to the twentieth and 21st centuries what discipline was to the eighteenth and nineteenth centuries, namely, an onto-historical formation of power and knowledge.

McKenzie, (2001)

The context in which England's policy on teaching is established has changed significantly over the last six decades. From the 1940s until the mid-1970s, teachers enjoyed a high degree of autonomy and trust in knowing what was best for pupils. From then until the 1980s the concept of accountability was introduced, under which management procedures replaced voluntary codes of professionalism. Local Management of Schools (LMS) was introduced, resulting in a shift of control from Local Education Authorities (LEAs) to individual schools. Subsequently, the government has introduced national league tables; national testing of pupils; publication of examination results; external inspections; and performance management. One of the collective effects of these initiatives has been to place the performance of teachers under the spotlight.

For the best part of twenty years, teachers in schools in England have experienced reform on an unprecedented scale. In central government's drive to raise standards in schools, it has implemented policies that have created pressures on teachers not only to improve their performance but also to sustain high levels of performance. The large majority of teachers have accommodated this reform with characteristic good humour – at times, tinged with healthy scepticism but also with a determination to make things work for the benefit of the pupils they teach. Others, it has to be said, have found it more difficult to cope with the array of initiatives and have, for a number of reasons, under-performed.

Under-performance among teachers presents an enormous challenge for leaders and managers in education at all levels, despite improvements in staff selection and training and the existence of national standards for teachers. Teacher under-performance is not new of course – many teachers, like many workers in other fields, under-perform at some time, and in some contexts. Each of the writers of this book very quickly recounted the influence of under-performing teachers on their own learning as pupils. We were also honest enough to confess that there had been times in our own teaching careers (not many!) when – for all sorts of reasons – we had also under-performed.

So why has our awareness of teachers' under-performance risen in recent years. There are a number of reasons, many of which stem from a growing demand from central government for teachers to be made more accountable for what goes on in their teaching areas. Two prominent, government-initiated, initiatives that have increased this level of accountability have been Ofsted inspections and performance management. Fullan and Hargreaves (1992) suggest that:

> *If you open up classrooms to find excellence, you also risk exposing bad practice and incompetence. While this risk is real, the actual scale of the incompetence problem is smaller than the fears to which it gives rise.*

Nor is the question of teacher quality just an issue for the United Kingdom – all countries are seeking to improve their schools. An Organisation for Economic Co-operation and Development (OECD) report entitled *Teachers Matter: Attracting, Developing and Retaining Effective Teachers* (OECD, 2005) focuses on policies that contribute to attracting, developing and retaining effective teachers in schools. The report draws on the results of a major OECD study of teacher policy conducted over the 2002–04 period in collaboration with 25 countries around the world.

> *As the most significant and costly resource in schools, teachers are central to school improvement efforts. Improving the efficiency and equity of schooling depends, in large measure, on ensuring that competent people want to work as teachers, that their teaching is of high quality, and that all students have access to high quality teaching.*
>
> (OECD, 2005)

Teachers who under-perform not only fail to achieve expected results, but their behaviour may also have a deleterious effect on the work of others. They consume much of school leadzers' time and occupy posts that would be better filled by better performing teachers. Their ineffective performance may also damage the school's reputation – often raising fierce reaction from parents. The continued emphasis by Ofsted on raising standards of teaching and learning puts pressure on individual teachers, and those managing them, to ensure that any weaknesses in classroom performance are remedied.

Why has this book been written?

This book has been written in the belief that it will help teachers, and those managing their performance, to develop further strategies and improve current ones in order to correct weaknesses in their practice. This is intended to be essentially a practical book for busy senior and middle managers in primary, middle and secondary schools who are required to manage and, wherever possible, reverse the under-performance of those with whom they work. It is intended that much of the material found in the book will also help under-performing staff to reflect upon and improve their performance.

It is crucial to point out that this book is not about teachers whose performance has deteriorated so significantly that, despite quality support, capability procedures are called for. Its emphasis is on those teachers who are, in general, capable but have significant weaknesses in a number of critical aspects of their work – '*they fall below a threshold of satisfactory performance on a number of criteria: they are not just unsatisfactory in one small aspect of the job*' (Fidler and Atton, 1999).

The structure of the book

In Chapter 1 we look at some fundamental questions associated with the under-performance of teachers and present a series of issues that need serious consideration. The chapter describes the consequences for schools of teacher under-performance and attempts to clarify what we mean by under-performance within the context of what we know about teacher effectiveness.

In Chapter 2 the authors draw upon their experience to look more closely at the nature of ineffective or poor performance in teachers. It highlights the use of supporting benchmarks to help draw distinctions between performance that can be restored and that which inevitably leads to capability procedures and possible dismissal.

Chapter 3 focuses on the practical support strategies that line-managers can put in place to improve and restore teachers' professional practice. Teachers who are under-performing will need a programme of structured support, individually tailored to take account of the balance between individual, immediate and wider context issues which have given rise to the poor performance.

The aim of Chapter 4 is to examine the role of self-reflection in improving teacher effectiveness, to prompt and extend self-reflection for teachers who are already self-reflective, and to provide assistance to line-managers who need to encourage self-reflection in teachers being supported to become more effective.

Chapter 5 focuses on the potential of performance reviews to reverse the trend of under-performance amongst some teachers through their emphasis on planning priorities, forming objectives and individual improvement plans, and on appropriate support and challenge. We advocate coaching as an essential skill for team leaders in supporting under-performing teachers. It describes the challenge for team leaders in confronting unacceptable practice and identifies strategies for giving constructive criticism. It emphasises the need for early intervention and for team leaders to be aware of equality issues in their own judgements and behaviour. The importance of giving high quality feedback is highlighted in order to effect change and enable the recipient to retain a sense of self-worth and self-fulfilment.

In Chapter 6 we suggest a whole-school approach to maintaining and developing teacher performance further through the use of a Professional Development Group.

The importance of sound recruitment and selection procedures in making the right appointments is covered in Chapter 7. It provides a comprehensive strategy for preparing for a selection process with substantial guidance on securing the best candidates to fill vacancies.

We use Chapter 8 as a resource made up of authentic case study materials that readers might use to consolidate their learning and plan appropriate action to help restore the performance of teachers. The materials are also provided to support in-school training events on the issues surrounding supporting under-performing teachers.

The challenge to schools posed by under-performing teachers

This chapter sets the scene for the rest of the book's contents by discussing key questions raised by the issue of teacher under-performance in schools. The issues raised are revisited, in greater detail, in later chapters of the book.

What are the consequences for schools of teacher under-performance?

It has been said before and, in all probability, it will be said time and time again – the single most significant factor in a child's learning is the teacher. Haim Ginott's (1972) famous quote reminds us of the power that lies in the hands of teachers:

> *I have come to a frightening conclusion. I am the decisive element in the classroom. It is my personal approach that creates the climate. It is my daily mood that makes the weather. As a teacher I possess tremendous power to make a child's life miserable or joyous. I can be a tool of torture or an instrument of inspiration. I can humiliate or humour, hurt or heal. In all situations, it is my response that decides whether a crisis will be escalated or de-escalated, and a child humanized or de-humanized.*

Pupils have a remarkable flair for both recognising and valuing teachers whose enthusiasm shines through their teaching and whose high-order communication skills can be witnessed in every interaction they share. Given the weight of reform that teachers now carry, it is to their enormous credit that so many continue to bring this professionalism to bear on their work. A survey by Wragg *et al.* (2000) sums up the context of a teacher's current role as follows:

During the last few years of the twentieth century there were many factors which combined to demand from teachers even higher levels of professional competence. They included the rapid growth in the acquisition of knowledge; the changing nature . . . of adult employment . . .; greatly increased public pressure for accountability, accompanied by numerous demands and changes to curriculum, assessment and conditions of service; the development of new forms of educational, information and communication technology and the ever broadening role of the teacher, with demands on skill spilling over into other professional fields like 'administrator', 'social worker' and 'manager'.

It is not surprising, therefore, that some teachers do not cope with the demands made of them, with the result that their performance begins to deteriorate. Under-performing teachers present one of the most difficult challenges school leaders may ever encounter. Dean's (2002) observation is that:

The headteacher and team leader see that pupils are getting a raw deal and hate the task of setting out to deal with the problem. Yet, such problems will not go away and such teachers do not always respond to support and encouragement.

Teachers who perform inadequately not only fail to achieve their own performance standards, but they can also affect the performance of those with whom they come into contact, e.g. other staff, pupils. Teachers' under-performance can have a negative impact upon the:

- school's reputation and standing in the community;
- attainment and achievements of pupils;
- performance of other teachers;
- performance of support staff; and
- leadership and management of the school.

With so much at stake, head teachers are understandably anxious about having to deal with these situations. As one head teacher commented:

Dealing with an ineffective teacher is the hardest thing a head ever does. You have to make yourself unpopular and you face the danger that the teacher will enlist support from other colleagues and you end up with a split in the school.

(Wragg et al., 2000)

Yet, to do nothing is to endanger the educational opportunities of many pupils and waste investment in the costliest resource any school has – its staff. It is also important not to underestimate the impact of this situation on the individual teacher. Invariably, the teacher loses self-esteem and confidence when placed in these circumstances. The longer this situation is allowed to continue without remediation, the more difficult it is to restore that teacher's performance.

How is performance and under-performance defined?

It is difficult to arrive at a precise meaning of under-performance without first defining what is meant by 'performance'. Armstrong (2000) maintains that 'if performance cannot be defined, it can't be measured or managed'. Bates and Holton (1995) underline the term's complexity when they describe performance as a 'multi-dimensional construct, the measurement of which varies depending on a variety of factors'.

Not surprisingly, there seems to be no universal agreement on what the term 'performance' means. However, as can be seen from the following definitions and descriptions, several researchers have attempted to add their contributions to our understanding:

> *. . . it is a record of a person's accomplishments.*
>
> (Armstrong, 2000)
>
> *. . . something that the person leaves behind and that exists apart from the purpose.*
>
> (Kane, 1996)
>
> *. . . the outcomes of work because they provide the strongest linkage to the strategic goals of the organisation, customer satisfaction, and economic contribution.*
>
> (Bernadin et al., 1995)
>
> *. . . the accomplishment, execution, carrying out, working out of anything ordered or undertaken.*
>
> (*Oxford Education Dictionary*)

This latter definition refers to the achievement of outputs and outcomes, while also emphasising the importance of actually doing the work. Individuals' performance could therefore be regarded as the way in which they get tasks (e.g. teaching, marking, assessments) done.

A dilemma faced by writers on the subject is whether to distinguish between the *behaviour* of performing from the *outcomes* of performance. Brumbach (1988) offers a more comprehensive view of performance by attempting to embrace both behaviour and outcomes. For him:

> *Performance means both behaviours and results. Behaviours emanate from the performer and transform performance from abstraction to action.*

3

Not just the instruments for results, behaviours are also outcomes in their own right – the product of mental and physical effort applied to tasks – and can be judged apart from results.

This definition of performance leads to the conclusion that an individual's performance needs to be gauged with both behaviours and outcomes in mind.

Fidler and Atton (1999) chose to use the term 'poor performers' for employees who are not performing satisfactorily, stressing the point that such employees have major failings in a number of critical aspects of their work: 'They fall below a threshold of satisfactory performance on a number of criteria: they are not just unsatisfactory in one small aspect of the job'. Implied here is the existence of a recognisable benchmark that can be used to determine minimum satisfactory performance. So, where do we find benchmarks? What are appropriate benchmarks for gauging the effectiveness of teachers' performance?

What is now known about teacher effectiveness?

Teacher effectiveness has attracted particularly close scrutiny as part of the government's drive to raise the quality of teaching and learning and, therefore, school standards. Attempts to define the skills, knowledge and attributes required by effective teachers to help them review their performance and to support them in their continuing professional development are signs of the government's strategy to manage the teaching force.

The research commissioned from Hay/McBer by the, then, Department for Education and Employment (DfEE) was designed to provide a framework describing effective teaching. They set out to develop a clear description of teacher effectiveness, based on evidence of what effective teachers do in practice at different stages in the profession.

Effective teachers in the future will need to deal with a climate of continual change in which distance learning and other teaching media will become more prevalent. The 'star teachers' of the future will be those who work to make what is now the best become the standard for all. School managers will need to create a school climate that fosters a framework for continuous improvement. One critical dimension is likely to be openness to the integration of good practice from other teachers, schools, regions or even countries. This will require a shift in culture so that real team working is valued, and mutual feedback – through lesson observation or other means – is embraced as an essential part of professional development.

(Hay/McBer, 2000)

Recent research reveals that the greatest impact on overall school effectiveness is due to classroom-level factors, rather than school-level factors. For these reasons, attempting to identify what makes an effective teacher has become an important feature within the recognised research community. Muijs and Reynolds (2005), for example, conclude that effective teachers:

- have a positive attitude;
- develop a pleasant social/psychological climate in the classroom;
- have high expectations of what pupils can achieve;
- communicate lesson clarity;
- practise effective time management;
- employ strong lesson structuring;
- use a variety of teaching methods;
- use and incorporate pupil ideas; and
- use appropriate and varied questioning.

However, they remind us that effective teaching methods are context specific. What is needed for a teacher to be effective can vary depending upon factors such as:

- the type of activity in the lesson;
- the subject matter;
- the pupil backgrounds (such as age, ability, gender, socio-economic status and ethnicity);
- the pupils' personal characteristics (such as personality, learning style, motivation and self-esteem); and
- the culture/organisation of the department, school and LEA.

How is teacher under-performance recognised?

Given the significant findings of research into essentially 'what makes a good teacher?', together with the increasing exposure of school practices and achievements to the public, it is relatively easy to identify teachers who are under-performing. Rather more difficult to gauge is the extent to which the under-performance is prolonged and consistent. Among the key means of identifying teacher under-performance are the following:

- feedback from external inspection (Ofsted);
- the outcomes of self-review and moderated self-review procedures;
- self-perceived problems;
- the outcomes of performance management reviews;
- scrutiny of pupil progress data;
- informal monitoring by middle and senior leaders;
- monitoring by local authority for school improvement;

- escalating disruptive pupil behaviour;
- lesson observations; and
- complaints from pupils, parents, other staff, etc.

Given the increased attention being given to teacher under-performance, the reader might be forgiven for believing that teacher under-performance is a relatively new phenomenon. We suspect not – the transparency of school practices has meant that under-performers are more easily detected these days and there is a greater pressure on school leaders to address teacher under-performance for the reasons set out earlier.

However, there remains a tendency for some school leaders to avoid direct conflict and dispensing painful criticism. Managers, as Schaffer (1991) points out, sometimes use a variety of psychological ploys for avoiding the unpleasant truth that gaps in performance exist. These ploys include:

- **Evasion through rationalisation**
  Managers try to convince themselves that they have done everything possible to establish expectations. They are too ready to accept claims of overload, accusations that the system is to blame, and may even compensate for poor performance by taking on extra work themselves to mask any shortfall.
- **Reliance on procedures**
  Managers may rely on a variety of procedures, programmes and systems to produce better results, sit back and wait for them to take effect without making a sustained effort to address the precise issues that cause the underperformance.
- **Attacks that skirt the target**
  Managers may set tough goals and insist that they are achieved, but they may still fail to produce a sense of accountability from individuals whose performance is under scrutiny. Following their research, Fidler and Atton (1999), helpfully, categorise under-performance as either 'long standing' or 'having recently appeared'. They maintain that there is a greater degree of difficulty in dealing with under-performance depending on whether the situation is recent or long standing.

Studies by Parry (1991) in the United States and Wragg et al. (2000) in the United Kingdom found that a teacher may demonstrate under-performance in a number of ways:

- inability to control the class;
- poor planning and preparation;
- poor subject knowledge;
- poor teaching;
- low expectations of pupils;
- poor relationships with pupils;

- poor relationships with colleagues;
- poor quality pupil learning and progress;
- lack of commitment to the work; and
- inability or unwillingness to respond to change.

What are the causes of teacher under-performance?

According to Armstrong (2000): 'poor performance may be the result of inadequate leadership, bad management or defective systems of work'. He goes on to say that: 'All are probably the result of a failure of whoever is at the top of the organization to establish well-defined and unequivocal expectations for superior performance'.

Table 1.1, adapted by Rhodes and Beneicke (2003) from the work of Weightman (1999), illustrates likely areas of critical under-performance among teachers. It offers a framework to facilitate manager/teacher analysis of the causes of poor performance. Individual teachers and their line-managers will find the framework helpful in reflecting on the possible causes of under-performance.

Following their research, Fidler and Atton (1999) identified the following causes of teacher under-performance:

- the job and its context;
- the way in which the employee has been managed;
- the selection and appointment of the employee; and
- the employee.

Who should take responsibility for dealing with teacher under-performance?

The development of a teacher's performance, ideally as part of a continuous process of performance management, needs to be tackled at both the school and the individual level. To avoid having to take action to deal with teachers who are not up to standard through capability procedures, the aim should be to be positive about minimising under-performance.

It would be nice to think that all teachers are sufficiently professional and reflective about their practice. The majority are, and others have strived to become, outstanding practitioners because of their willingness and ability to reflect critically on their practice and to make the necessary improvements. Often, this reflection has been supported and informed by peers, for example colleagues adopting the roles of mentor, coach and critical friend.

Table 1.1 *Possible causes of poor performance (Rhodes and Beneicke (2003) after Weightman (1999))*

Possible causes	Organisational problems	Management problems	Team problems	Post holder problems	Personal problems
Structure	Structure too complex.	Poor communication.	Destructive group dynamics.	Changes may not make sense to individual.	Transport/Location difficulties. Domestic arrangements incompatible with job.
Systems	Inappropriate personnel systems and practices.	Inappropriate support and control.	Personality clashes.	Lack of appropriate guidelines.	Confusion.
Role	Job/Role ill defined.	Unclear objectives. Inadequate performance appraisal.	Divergent team roles.	Confusion over job/role.	Lack of motivation.
Development	Lack of planning.	Lack of individually focused training.	Lack of team development.	Poor job/skill fit. Lack of appropriate training.	Intellectual ability inappropriate to current job.
Resources	Inadequate physical resources.	Perceived bias or injustice in resource allocation.	Power struggles.	Unrealistic expectations with respect to time for task completion.	Technical skills inadequate. Demotivation.
Leadership	Individuals do not appear to be valued.	Inconsistent, inadequate leadership.	Inconsistent, inadequate team leadership. Conflict of views and values.	Unclear objectives.	Confusion. Disregard for health, family or personal problems.

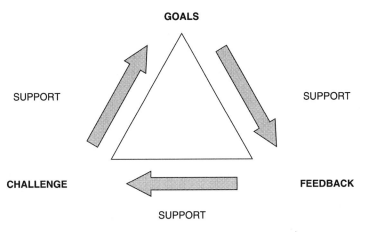

Figure 1.1 *A proposed model for managing teacher under-performance*

How can performance management be used to tackle under-performance?

The improvement of performance as part of a continuous process of performance management needs to be tackled at both the organizational and the individual level.

(Armstrong, 2000)

A number of reasons may contribute to a teacher's under-performance at any point in time. These reasons may relate to inadequate leadership, indifferent management practices or defective systems and procedures. Ultimately, senior leaders in schools will need to consider whether there are sufficiently well-defined expectations for high-order performance. Performance management is not just about offering support; it is also about providing appropriate challenge. To have any chance of success, managing under-performance must be regarded as a positive process, employing the model shown in Figure 1.1.

This model relies heavily on regular and systematic feedback to the teacher by understanding and competent colleagues. Furthermore, these colleagues (usually at middle and senior leadership level within the school) should have a thorough knowledge of:

- the teacher's role and responsibilities;
- the teacher's current performance standards;
- reasons for the shortfall in performance; and
- techniques, ploys and systems that could be employed by the teacher to overcome performance difficulties.

Before introducing strategies for reversing under-performance, it is important to understand the factors that influence motivation, the necessity for early intervention in situations where behaviour or practice is unacceptable, the skills needed for sensitive confrontation of difficulties, and to know about and practise strategies for giving constructive criticism.

People, including teachers, have a basic need to know how well they are doing. One of the acknowledged benefits of performance management is the opportunity it provides to recognise the teacher's work and contribution to the school. In this respect, praise and celebration of success are powerful motivators. Research such as *Milestone or Millstone? Performance Management in Schools: Reflections on the Experiences of Industry* (Industry in Education, 2000) shows that:

- professional staff welcome feedback on their overall performance; and
- a significant benefit of participation in performance reviews arises from the existence of the feedback process itself, i.e. the awareness of doing, and being seen to be doing, a good job.

Motivation and effort increase when the goals are achievable – decrease when perceived as unachievable. The challenge for team leaders is to motivate teachers whose performance falls below an acceptable level. They need to be able to:

- give criticism constructively – positive reinforcement of an acceptable behaviour increases the chance that that behaviour will be repeated;
- enable teachers to confront under-performance and to acknowledge that improvement is needed;
- agree appropriate action; and
- identify success criteria and timescale, including monitoring activities.

A guiding principle should always be that under-performance is identified and dealt with immediately.

Recognising teacher under-performance

In this chapter, the authors draw on their experience of under-performing teachers in a wide variety of schools, to look more closely at the nature of teacher under-performance. Teachers, and their line-managers, need to be able to identify the elements of under-performance as the first stage of the process of recovering and restoring a professionally acceptable standard of performance on the part of the individual teacher. This involves consideration of national standards for effective performance and Ofsted criteria for unsatisfactory and poor teaching, plus a consideration of different types of ineffectiveness and an analysis of the location of factors contributing to ineffective or unsatisfactory performance.

Constituents of teacher under-performance

What does teacher under-performance look like? How does it differ from satisfactory or better performance? How inadequate does the teacher have to be before some remedial action has to be taken? Her Majesty's Chief Inspector of Schools (HMCI) (Ofsted, 2004) found teaching unsatisfactory or worse in 5% of secondary schools and 3% of primary schools in England but, even where schools had good Ofsted inspection reports, there are often references to the need for managers to tackle 'the few remaining shortcomings in teaching' (Ofsted, 2004).

For those who wish to reflect on their own practice and also for those who line-manage teachers, e.g. team leaders, middle managers, key stage co-ordinators, heads of department, and who are accountable for their performance, it is important to be able to clearly identify and diagnose the nature and the extent of the teacher's under-performance. Before deciding that there is evidence of under-performance, it may be helpful to look at the:

- Professional Standards for Teachers; and
- criteria associated with the Ofsted inspection process.

Professional standards for teachers

The professional standards have been in existence since the late 1990s and are currently being revised by the Training and Development Agency (TDA) in areas such as: Qualified Teacher Status (QTS), induction, senior teacher (threshold), and Advanced Skills Teacher (AST).

It is helpful to look at these professional standards to obtain a clear idea of the standards that teachers in the modern profession should be reaching and aspiring to. This can help to give teachers and their line-managers a benchmark against which to gauge their effectiveness. They can also be used as an aid to self-reflection and as a prompt for line-managers to focus their thinking on the performance of individual teachers.

Point for reflection

Read the professional standards relating to QTS and use a rating of 1–5 (5 being good and 1 being very poor) to score either your own performance or the performance of a teacher about whom you have concerns. This approach can be used with any of the professional standards that are relevant to the teacher concerned.

Ofsted inspection criteria

Having considered the national standards, it may now be helpful to look at how Ofsted inspectors recognise effective and ineffective teaching.

The quality of teaching must be judged first and foremost in terms of its effect on learning. Effective teaching reflects the commitment and determination of all staff to ensure that every pupil succeeds. It requires methods that engage pupils in productive learning, the imagination to make learning vivid and relevant, and the skill to build on what pupils know and to evaluate how well they are achieving.

(Ofsted, 2003a; 2003b)

Ofsted summarises unsatisfactory teaching and learning in primary and secondary schools in similar terms (see Table 2.1).

The inspection handbooks make it clear that teaching and/or learning cannot be described as satisfactory if any of the elements described in Table 2.1 are present. This can be presented as a checklist for identifying unsatisfactory teaching:

Table 2.1   *Ofsted's summary of unsatisfactory teaching and learning*

Unsatisfactory in secondary schools
Significant proportions of pupils make limited progress and underachieve. Teaching is dull and fails to capture pupils' interest and enthusiasm or does not indicate the curriculum has been adjusted well enough to facilitate access. Activities are mundane and, because of limited tuning to individuals' needs, some pupils get little from them. Greater effort is directed towards managing behaviour than learning. At times weak behaviour is exacerbated. Some pupils are easily distracted and lack the motivation to work. Staff have an incomplete understanding of areas of learning, subjects or courses, resulting in patchy coverage. Too little regard is paid to the priority needs of pupils. Teachers' sights may be set too low and they may accept pupils' efforts too readily. Support staff provide an extra pair of hands, but little effective support for learning

---

Point for reflection

In relation to a lesson taught by you or a colleague, pose the following questions in an attempt to isolate both positive and negative elements of the lesson.

Are any of the following features present in the teaching observed?	Yes/No
Significant proportions of pupils make limited progress and underachieve.	
Teaching is dull and fails to capture pupils' interest and enthusiasm.	
Teaching does not indicate that the curriculum has been adjusted well enough to facilitate access.	
Activities are mundane and because of limited tuning to individuals' needs, some pupils get little from them.	

(Continued)

(Continued)

Greater effort is directed towards managing behaviour than learning.	
At times weak behaviour is exacerbated.	
Some pupils are easily distracted and lack the motivation to work.	
Staff have an incomplete understanding of areas of learning, subjects or courses resulting in patchy coverage.	
Too little regard is paid to the priority needs of pupils.	
Teachers' sights may be set too low and they may accept pupils' efforts too readily.	
Support staff provide an extra pair of hands, but little effective support for learning.	
If any of these factors are present, the lesson is unsatisfactory	

Point for reflection

Read the following description of a lesson observed in a secondary school and use the table above to decide whether or not it is an unsatisfactory lesson. If you think this lesson is satisfactory, what further advice would you offer to the teacher?

The teacher arrived at the lesson 5 minutes after the scheduled start of the lesson with a Year 9 Maths group in the ICT room. She wrote the lesson objectives on the board. These were clear but were not levelled. There was a lengthy recapitulation of the content covered during the previous lesson during which some pupils became very restless.

The pupils were then asked to log onto their computers but there were technical hitches with some of the machines and the technician had to be sent for to sort these out which delayed the start of the first activity.

(Continued)

The pupils who had to wait to log on had nothing immediately to do and began shouting across the room to their friends. The teacher got deflected from teaching the rest of the group into managing the behaviour of these pupils. However, she showed good behaviour management skills, remaining calm but insistent that the behaviour was not acceptable.

The lesson continued with a good selection of different tasks to suit most learners in the group. The teacher attempted to get pace into the lesson by giving the pupils timed activities but the timings were too short for most pupils to manage and a few pupils became frustrated and drifted off task. Others responded well to this approach and made real learning gains.

The lesson finished with a question and answer session but all the questions were closed questions and pupils were not encouraged to pose questions for themselves. The end of the lesson was rushed and there was not an orderly dismissal from the room as pupils were anxious to catch the end of day buses.

Analysing ineffective teaching

Fidler and Atton (1999) used the euphemism 'poor performers' to cover the range of teachers whose work might be categorised as ineffective, and defined these as teachers who 'have major failings in a number of critical aspects of their work'. Stoll and Myers (1998) looked at the language used to describe failing schools and identified: failing, ineffective, underachieving, schools with problems, struggling, troubled, troubling, swaying, stuck, sinking, sliding, cruising and promenading. Similarly, the authors of this book have found a range of negative descriptive terms for teachers who are not performing in line with the national standards for QTS or in line with Ofsted expectations of satisfactory or better teaching. These teachers can be described as: ineffective, struggling, under-performing, sliding, sinking, stuck, or incapable. Despite the negativity of the terms, there is perhaps a suggestion in Table 2.2 of some differentiation of performance or situation in terms of the language used.

This book is concerned with the five categories of teacher ineffectiveness listed in the table since all of these, arguably, represent teachers who have not yet reached the point where it is appropriate to follow capability procedures to remove them from the teaching profession.

Stoll and Myers (1998) link the language used to describe failing schools with the 'culture of blame' and add that the notion of 'zero tolerance of failure' suggests that 'this is not an option and that we must turn away from, reject, punish and blame those who fail'. Similarly, there might be a view that teachers who are demonstrating symptoms of ineffectiveness are entirely to blame and that the response should be a similar zero-tolerance approach. In this book, we argue for the importance of restorative approaches for the large majority of those who can be categorised as having unsatisfactory performance. Given the perceived difficulties for senior managers of embarking on capability procedures and their reluctance to do so, it could be argued that a commitment to restorative approaches is the best hope for those on the receiving end of poor teaching and learning.

While it may be easy to point the finger directly at the under-performing teacher, it can be argued that such teachers present a range of symptoms that can be located in a number of different areas relating to the:

- individual teacher;
- immediate working context; and
- wider school context.

Individual difficulties

These difficulties usually stem from an individual's personality, upbringing and training. As such, they may be deep-seated and tricky to change. However, being aware of them can at least help a line-manager to understand the individual teacher better. A consideration of personality raises a complex mix of genetic, behavioural, social, cultural and other influences and it would be understandable if a line-manager chose to abandon any action on the basis that the teacher 'is just like that' and:

Table 2.2   *Differentiated terms for under-performing teachers*

Ineffective teachers	• have poor pedagogic practices and/or poor relationships with pupils; • are unaware of the contribution they personally must make to improving their practice and approach with pupils and tend to blame external factors (the pupils, the parents, the school's managers, etc.) for their difficulties.
Struggling teachers	• have many of the poor practices of the ineffective teacher but are trying to find ways of improving their practice; • may be spasmodic or misguided in their attempts but there is a spark of self-reflection in their approach; • are likely to be NQTs or teachers new to a particular post or a particular school who are struggling to develop the range of skills and approaches they need for their new role.
Under-performing teachers (viewed by some as the equivalent to 'cruising schools')	• have the ability but do not push themselves to the limits of their capacity; • are likely to be adequate in most classroom situations but contribute nothing to the wider life of the school; • are in danger of becoming 'stuck' teachers as they do nothing to update their skills and approaches.
Sinking teachers	• are those who were (probably) once satisfactory teachers who have lost their way; • may be suffering from 'burn out', have external life problems which are deflecting their energies and commitment away from teaching, or have medical or psychological difficulties; • are often long-serving teachers who have worked in one institution for many years; • usually have discipline problems, but are increasingly resistant to new approaches; • may have the potential to be reflective practitioners but increasingly have less inclination to be so.
Stuck teachers	• are teachers who have not moved on and adapted to the changing demands of teaching; • employ pedagogic practices that are located in a time warp (e.g. dictated notes, copying from the board, rote learning); • view teacher–pupil relationships as ones based upon automatic respect for the teacher and show a lack of empathy with the view point of the pupil; • often have discipline problems brought about by their teaching style and level of expectation.

'change is not possible. However, some social psychologists argue that 'there is actually very little evidence for stable personality traits. People behave in different ways at different times and in different contexts – they are influenced by situation and context'.

(Hogg and Vaughan, 2005)

If this is correct, it reinforces the views expressed in this book that, where a teacher is under-performing, the teacher's line-manager should take action to help the individual to learn more appropriate self-management techniques, behaviours in the classroom, etc. Furthermore, our premise is that it is possible for all individuals to make some changes in an effort to improve upon current practice.

Point for reflection

Read the following account and consider the extent to which the difficulties experienced by this teacher are the result of his/her personal approach.

In the staff-room, the teacher kept up a constant litany of negative remarks about the pupils s/he taught. S/he referred to pupils as 'animals' and often brought individual pupils personally to senior managers clearly expecting that senior managers would back him/her without question and that the pupil would undergo a form of ritual humiliation. The senior manager would be informed loudly that 'this pupil does not know how to behave' and, whether he or she wanted it or not, the senior manager then received a slow but unstoppably detailed account of the pupil's crimes from the point of view of the teacher. Even when the pupils had calmed down, this deliberate and relentless repetition of their crimes, without any opportunity to put their side of the matter, often drove pupils into further confrontation. The teacher appeared to be oblivious to the effect that s/he had and even when explicitly asked by senior managers to discontinue this practice, carried on doing so.

An individual's personality, upbringing and training can also affect the nature of the relationship s/he develops in the classroom. Some teachers appear to have difficulties in creating the right kind of professional relationships with pupils – they are too stern, too kind, too unforgiving, too demanding, too lax or too inconsistent in their approach. This often results in pupils finding it hard to relate to them and becoming disruptive. Often, the individual teacher can appear to lack a clear view of what a professional relationship with pupils should look like. Instead of considering objectively what a teaching relationship might look like, these teachers sometimes replicate relationships they have personally experienced as pupils themselves.

In observing a teacher in the classroom and looking at the nature of the relationships with pupils, it is helpful to identify where power is located and how it is being used. For example, a teacher replicating a submissive relationship she has experienced may, for example, cede power to the pupils, choosing to be a 'facilitator' and to shy away from any approach that requires her to be the dominant figure in the classroom. Alternatively, a teacher who feels insecure about his social relationships may cling to power and act in an authoritarian and domineering manner.

Point for reflection

Read the following account and consider what you would say to this teacher about her professional relationship with pupils.

The art teacher liked to be one of 'the crowd'. She cultivated friendships with members of her teaching groups by bringing in family photographs and sometimes telling them intimate details of her personal life. Her teaching method was to have the pupils clustered around her so that social chat could take place as they did their art work. Her lessons were spontaneous with a strong emphasis on 'getting alongside' the pupils. Her classroom language, dress and approach were informal and pupils responded by freely telling her their problems both in the lesson and outside it. Resources had to be accessed through the teacher, who liked individuals to appear dependent on her. She liked to 'be there' for her pupils, encouraging them to share problems and confidences and acting fiercely in their defence when 'her guys' were in trouble with other teachers. She often had behavioural problems with older boys in her class but rarely reported her difficulties to her line-manager. However, attention had been turned onto her after two incidents where pupils had been injured in her lesson. In the first instance, a girl had been hit in the eye by a book thrown across the room by another pupil and in the second a pupil had been stabbed by another pupil with a compass and had required first aid. Her Head of Year had also been concerned by an incident earlier in the year when she had allowed some Year 11 boys to make racist and sexually offensive comments in one lesson and had then told them off and sent them to the Head of Year for doing the same in another lesson.

In these cases, it may be helpful to get the teachers to focus on what a professional relationship with pupils should look like so that they have a stronger model to compare with their own practice. This can be done by arranging for the teachers to observe the practices of colleagues who model good professional relationships with their pupils. However, it may be necessary to provide the teachers with prompts for their observation to enable them to 'see' it.

Point for reflection

Teachers signal the fact that they wish to establish a professional relationship with pupils in a variety of spoken/unspoken, explicit and implicit ways. Observe a teacher's behaviour closely and identify the behaviours used.

Observation sheet: relationships in the classroom	
What does the teacher do to establish that the classroom is the teacher's space and that everyone is here to work? • Greeting pupils at the door/as they enter. • Insistence on start of lesson routine, e.g. books/pens on desk ready to begin. • Adopting an assertive stance (posture, eye contact, gestures, language) in the classroom where pupil behaviour on entering and settling can be monitored. • A seating plan. • Other (specify).	**Observations**
What does the teacher do to check or limit off-task behaviour? • Eye contact. • Personal gesture to pupil. • Praising on-task behaviour of others. • Reminder of classroom rules and redirection of an individual. • Use of assertive language ('that is not the way we behave here; choose a better way, thanks').	

(Continued)

How does the teacher handle dissent or non-compliance? • Avoidance of entering into an argument which puts the teacher on the same level as the pupil. • Partial agreement with insistence ('yes I understand you are tired but we need to complete this'). • Insistence with encouragement ('come on, you can do it'). • Insistence with staged sanctions and guaranteed action.	
How does the teacher interact with the pupils in the classroom? Which of the following can you see? • Humour. • Mutual respect. • Use of rewards and praise. • Teacher aware of individuals' concerns and issues (showing interest in pupils as individuals). • Boundary management (actions which reinforce that the teacher is in control and the pupils need to focus on their work). • Other (specify).	
What does the teacher do at the end of the lesson to reinforce the idea that pupils are here to learn and that it is the teacher's role to ensure that they do? • Plenary to reinforce learning. • Insistence on routines for tidying classroom and resources. • Exit routines (farewells, quick learning checks – 'tell me one thing you have learnt today'). • Other (specify).	

Other teachers experience difficulty because their training has not equipped them with a repertoire of skills to use in the classroom, or because they have developed unhelpful practices that have gone unchecked. If their basic training has not encouraged self-reflection for bringing about improvement, they may be reluctant to take risks or to attempt new methods and practices. These teachers need to acquire a 'tool kit' of skills and approaches that can be constantly updated throughout their careers. However, they may view attempts to encourage them to try new approaches as indirect and personal criticism and, as a result, may be highly resistant.

Immediate working context

Sometimes, the under-performance of teachers is brought about by the nature of their immediate working context. They may:

- be teaching in a cramped or inappropriately located room;
- have poor facilities;
- have limited access to resources;
- have no induction process;
- have unfriendly colleagues;
- have no access to further training; and
- have a weak line-manager.

In this context, some initial difficulties for a new or inexperienced member of staff can quickly escalate into significant problems. Teachers in this situation can feel disempowered and dispirited and may need considerable encouragement to try out new approaches and to request better facilities and resources.

Wider school context

For some under-performing teachers, difficulties can also arise when the wider context of the school fails to support or encourage them. Such schools are likely to demonstrate one or more of the following characteristics:

- the school's senior leadership and management is ineffectual;
- middle leaders are weak and ineffectual;
- the expectations of pupils and staff are depressed;
- systems for monitoring pupil behaviour are inadequate;
- systems for supporting teachers who are experiencing difficulties are non-existent or inadequate; and
- the commitment to staff training and development is low.

In the above scenario, under-performing teachers invariably 'go under'. If they are not sufficiently reflective themselves and eager to develop, in the absence of a coach or mentor that is caring for them, it is unlikely that their practice will improve. Teachers in this situation would be well advised to find one or more teachers on the staff whose practice they believe is good, observe what they do closely, and try to model themselves on the examples they set.

Point for reflection

Read the following account and identify features that make this a supportive whole-school climate for a teacher who is experiencing difficulties.

School A has an integrated system for monitoring pupil behaviour and providing support for teachers to manage the most difficult pupils. All staff have had training in the principles of assertive discipline and are expected to use a staged approach to managing poor behaviour. When a pupil reaches stage 3, a referral is written about the behaviour. The referral is sent to the school office where it is placed in the register for the form tutor to see within a day. The form tutor reinforces the school's disapproval of the behaviour and monitors the overall number of referrals received by any individual pupil. The referral slip is always passed on to the pastoral head and is returned to the school office where it is entered on a database. When a pupil receives several referrals, the form tutor makes a point of speaking to the pastoral head to arrange for the child's parents to come into school to discuss the situation.

Point for reflection

Consider the following account and analyse the extent to which the problems are located with the individuals, their immediate working context or the wider school context. Use Figure 2.1 to aid analysis.

Teacher A came from a very disciplined and cultured family background. He was the second son in a family of five. He struggled through his teacher training, often finding it difficult to find the time required to plan his lessons thoroughly. His first post was in a secondary school in a socially and economically deprived area. Here, he felt unsupported and alienated from the pupils he was allegedly teaching. After a year, he got a post in a school with a better social mix and looked forward to actually being able to teach. He was keen to make a new start but in his first few weeks he found it hard to get through lessons with older pupils without some disruptions. When pupils misbehaved, he sent them outside but often they caused more problems when there were several

(Continued)

(Continued)

of them outside the room than they had done when they were in the room. No one had told him about the school's discipline system and he had not had time to read the bulky handbook he had been given.

His Head of Department was also new to middle management responsibility. He had worked in the school for a number of years and had only applied for the post reluctantly. He felt anxious and uncertain in his new role, especially as he was following a powerful and well-respected Head of Department who had gone on to be a Deputy Head Teacher. He had no training for middle management and doubted his ability to match the performance of his predecessor. He was particularly worried about the need to modernise the existing schemes of work to incorporate cross-curricular themes, but did not want to admit his insecurity to anyone else in the school. He also had long-established friendships with other members of the department who were all members of the same sporting and social club, and their conversation at break and lunchtime related to these shared social activities. However, these friendships made it difficult for the new Head of Department to assert his authority within the department. The Head of Department was aware that the new teacher was having difficulties with some of his class and this had been discussed by the other members of the department informally with comments like 'why did you appoint him?' and 'can't he do anything?'

In this example, there are problems relating to the:

- individuals (lack of thorough preparation, use of inappropriate strategies for classroom management);
- immediate working context (a weak and unsupportive Head of Department, a close-knit group of colleagues who are quick to condemn rather than support);
- wider school context (a lack of a thorough induction process and a system for giving newcomers a 'mentor' outside their subject area).

Figure 2.1 provides a summary of the key factors that impact on a teacher's under-performance.

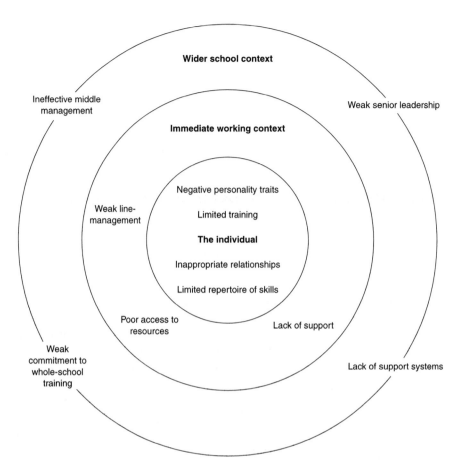

Figure 2.1   *Major influences on teachers' under-performance*

Supporting teachers to become more effective

Teachers who are not performing consistently in line with acceptable professional standards will need a programme of structured support, individually tailored, to take account of the individual, immediate and wider-context issues that may have given rise to the under-performance. In this chapter, the ways in which the need for support can be identified will be discussed, together with who should provide the support, and a description of a systematic support process.

Identifying the need for support

There are three ways in which the needs of individual teachers for additional support can be identified:

- self-identification;
- formal identification; and
- informal identification.

Self-identification

Ideally, teachers requiring additional support would identify this need themselves through reflection on their own practice and discussion with their line-manager or colleagues. However, one common feature of under-performing teachers is their lack of critical self-reflection and, in practice, teachers who are under-performing sometimes neither actively seek help nor engage in regular professional dialogue with their immediate line-manager or others to develop or enhance their skills. Despite their lack of self-reflection, teaching for these individuals is an intensely emotional activity, as it is for all teachers (James and Connolly, 2000).

Arguably, when powerful feelings of anxiety are created by a lesson that 'is not working', individual social defences can be deployed instead of self-reflection. Here, for example, the fear of losing control can be split off from the individual and projected onto the pupils in the classroom. Thus, it is the pupils – rather than the teacher – who have the problem of being out of control. This may explain why under-performing teachers have a tendency to blame pupils rather than look within themselves or analyse their own actions. Such teachers will often say, 'they don't know how to behave' or 'this boy can't behave', thus ignoring the uncomfortable evidence that the class or the individual *can* and *do* behave well in many situations. The key message here is that the actions of the teacher, whether in lesson planning or behaviour management, influences the behaviour of the pupils.

Formal identification

If the school has an effective performance management policy and appropriate procedures, ineffective performance should be identified by the relevant line-manager through lesson observation and other means, e.g. self-review systems. The analysis of examination and test results can also act as an indicator of problems. Clearly, teaching and learning are not input–output activities in which good teaching will automatically guarantee examination success, i.e. poor examination and test results are not always the result of poor teaching. However, when pupils do well, good teaching is likely to be one of the key contributing factors. It is important therefore that examination and test results are analysed to gauge whether problems exist in subject areas and to prompt further investigation into whether or not ineffective teaching is a cause.

Schools in England and Wales have access to increasingly sophisticated examination and test result analysis systems, including annual Performance and Assessment Data Analysis (PANDA) reports, that provide a range of performance analysis. LEAs provide schools with data enabling them to compare themselves with similar schools. Schools set pupils targets for academic progress based on the average progression from one stage to the next, and results can now be analysed in terms of the percentage of pupils who achieved these targets. For a variety of reasons, there will invariably be a small number of pupils who fail to reach their targets. However, if the performance of most of those being examined in a particular subject or key stage cohort is below target, then further explanations need to be sought, which might include the standard of teaching in that subject area.

Point for reflection

Consider the information presented in the latest PANDA report on the school and identify any subject areas where negative residuals indicate a need for further investigation and action.

Where negative residuals exist, it is important to try to establish the reasons for the under-performance in that subject area and to identify appropriate action.

Point for reflection

Consider this analysis of poor results in one curriculum area and decide whether the action plan addresses all the issues raised by the analysis.

Report from Head of History – annual examination analysis and action plan
Examination analysis shows:

- Pupils achieved on average two to three grades below their target grades.
- Boys are achieving higher grades than girls.
- Problems getting coursework from less motivated pupils had a negative impact on their results.
- Many of those who underachieved also did badly on the examined component of the course.

Action plan for improvement

- Start coursework earlier and provide a choice of topics which can cater for girls' interests better.
- Run after-school revision classes before the final examinations.

In the plan above, the issue of under-performing teachers was not confronted directly. In primary schools, an under-performing teacher can have an impact on a range of subject areas and the subject co-ordinator may have limited control of the teaching and learning methodologies employed in the classroom. Again, comparison of pupils' performance against their targets will give some idea of where the problem is located which can then prompt senior managers to take some action.

Informal identification

If self-reflection, performance management reviews or examination results analysis fail to identify problems; they normally emerge through more informal means, e.g. anecdotal evidence from pupils; feedback from Teaching Assistants (TAs) or other support staff; pupils being regularly sent out of a particular classroom or being referred to other staff for disciplining; and rising noise levels during lessons. Other signs of possible problems are: rowdy behaviour of pupils arriving from the previous lesson; an unsettled atmosphere in the classroom you are going into, possibly indicating that the previous learning experience has not been productive; misuse of resources (paper on the floor, chairs turned over, etc.). Parents may also pick up comments made by their child and his/her classmates and may contact the school either directly or through members of the governing body.

Who should provide support?

The culture of different schools varies. Some schools are very mutually supportive and develop a collegiate professional culture in which teachers naturally discuss how to improve their lessons or classroom management. Other schools have a more closed culture in which it is hard for an individual teacher to ask for, or to get, support. These differences apply as much to small primary schools as they do to large secondary schools.

Point for reflection

What advice would you offer to the member of staff described below?

A newly appointed Second in Department found it difficult to adapt the teaching and learning strategies she had used in her former employment in a high-performing middle-class school, to the demands of her new, much larger, more socially mixed school. She turned for support to the Head of Department, but he was a weak teacher who only taught the most able and sixth-form groups. He was unable to suggest any different strategies and gave the new teacher the impression that he thought she was a failure for asking him.

Support should be provided, and indeed should be offered initially, by those with a line-management responsibility for the individual teacher or for aspects of an individual teacher's work. This can be a senior manager, such as the head teacher or deputy, or a middle leader, such as a key stage co-ordinator or a head of department. However, if the support being provided is to stand a chance of working, it is crucial that the line-manager has professional credibility. Advice and guidance, however well meant, is unlikely to be accepted by an under-performing teacher if its source lacks credibility. An illustration of such a situation was seen recently in a primary school where the Deputy Head had been placed in charge of classroom standards, only to find that teachers rejected any advice given because s/he was viewed as a mediocre classroom practitioner.

If the school has good staff development and performance management policies and processes, it will be easier for both the line-manager and the individual teacher to embark on a programme of support. If these policies are less successful and the culture of the school is closed, the teacher should understand that s/he has a right to expect professional support and line-managers should be clear about their duty of care for other staff as well as their responsibility for standards of teaching and learning in their area. However, as the example above of a new teacher seeking help from a weaker Head of Department with a limited concept of his own role shows, the reality of the situation can be more difficult. In this case, the new teacher would be well advised to seek support from a teacher colleague whose expertise is widely acknowledged.

Point for reflection

If you have line-management responsibility for one or more members of teaching staff, consider the following checklist for each teacher you are responsible for:

Name of teacher: _____	Yes/No
Have you completed the teacher's annual performance management review?	
Has the teacher attended a recent professional development activity?	
Has the teacher had a satisfactory or better lesson observation this year?	
Are you aware of any difficulties of classroom management experienced by the teacher?	
Have you analysed the results produced by the teacher to identify any value-added problem?	

(Continued)

(Continued)

Are there any organisational, management or staffing issues which are having an impact on the teacher's performance?	
Are there any personal issues which are having an impact on the teacher's performance?	
Have there been any complaints from pupils, staff or parents about the teacher?	
Has the teacher asked for additional support?	

Once line-managers are aware that there are concerns about the performance of a teacher for whom they are responsible, they should have an initial discussion with the teacher to allow these concerns to be raised openly. At this stage it may be unclear whether the difficulties the teacher is experiencing relate to:

- pupil behaviours;
- teaching the schemes of work; or
- whole-school or key stage/subject area matters.

This initial discussion is the first stage of a process that will lead to a support plan being written for the teacher, regular reviews, and further support or other action to address the problem.

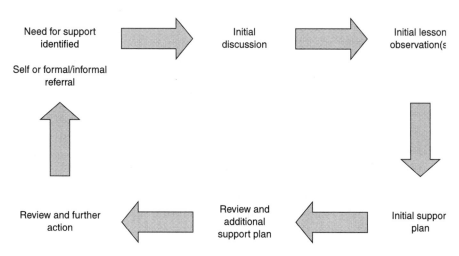

Figure 3.1 *The teacher support process*

The initial discussion

The discussion should focus on the concerns already raised about teaching performance and should clearly specify the line-manager's responsibility both to provide support and to ensure the quality of teaching and learning in their area of responsibility. This discussion needs to take place in a supportive but professional atmosphere. The teacher may already be defensive about the situation and it will be important not to give the individual any grounds for feeling harassed or victimised. This should not be a hurried conversation and certainly not held in the classroom where the teacher may be surrounded by pupils. The line-manager must take the time to create the right conditions for a productive professional discussion to take place.

Ideally the discussion would take place in an office or private area where there is less chance of interruption. It is helpful to think about the seating arrangement in order to avoid creating the impression that the member of staff is 'in trouble' and is being disciplined. The line-manager should use positive language and open, non-threatening body language but be prepared also to be assertive about the pupils' rights to have a good learning experience. Remember that a large part of what is meant is communicated non-verbally and avoid a harsh tone or an unsmiling look. Look for a 'win–win' resolution in which the teacher can accept support and the learning experience of the pupils can be improved.

You may find that in this initial discussion, the teacher blames the whole problem on individual pupils or groups of pupils. For example: '6F are the worst class I have ever taught. They are the group from hell and I have no control over them. They belong in a special school and I am not trained to teach pupils in a special school.' It is probably unhelpful at this stage to enter into a lengthy debate with the member of staff about the precise misdeeds of the class or individual pupils, although the teacher may need to 'vent' some anxieties and frustrations. The line-manager should attempt to focus on:

- clarifying why there are concerns;
- the nature of those concerns;
- stressing his/her own professional duty to provide support to the teacher; and
- gaining acceptance from the teacher that classroom observation may be needed to help establish a clearer picture of the support which would be most useful.

Point for reflection
Consider the following ways of initiating discussion with an under-performing teacher and decide which approach might be more successful.
Case 1 I have noticed that there are often boys sent out of your classroom when you teach 8C in the afternoon. A parent has contacted me to express some concerns about rowdy behaviour in this class. I would like to hear your views about this and I think we need to think of ways to support you if you are finding this class difficult.
Case 2 The TA (Teaching Assistant) in your classroom came to the Head Teacher. She feared for the health and safety of pupils because pencils and rubbers were being thrown around in the classroom and you appeared not to notice or to be able to control the situation. The Head Teacher was concerned about this and asked me to see you.

Difficulties with the initial discussion

Line-managers sometimes find it difficult to have this initial discussion, especially if they have worked with the teacher for a number of years, or if they are younger or newer to the organisation than the teacher. It is almost inevitable that teachers will experience some difficulty in accepting the fundamental notion that it is their personal practice that has to change to correct the situation. Line-managers must expect resistance and reaction, ranging from blaming others for the current state of affairs, total negativity, and denial, to unrealistic demands for the removal of one or two trouble-makers from a particular class to solve the problem. However, if this initial discussion is done in an open and professional way, it can encourage the start of a process of self-reflection, which is the key to professional development. The line-manager may agree to the temporary removal of one or two pupils as a means of showing immediate support and building rapport with the member of staff, but this must always be done in the context of stressing that these are the pupils that the teacher is employed to teach and, if they are indeed challenging, then the teacher must use the support available to develop new strategies to cope with them.

In some schools, line-managers may find themselves holding line-management responsibility for aspects of the work of a more senior member of staff. This can present particular challenges. However, the status of the under-performing teacher is no excuse for professional inactivity.

Point for reflection

What advice would you give to the middle leader described here?

The new Head of Department had a Deputy Head working in his department who was always late for her lessons. He spoke to her informally about this but the problem continued. He then asked the Head Teacher for advice. He advised him to collect evidence of the deputy's lateness and to invite her to a formal meeting to discuss it. The deputy sent the Head of Department a letter saying she had consulted her union and she could only be disciplined by a more senior member of staff. The Head of Department referred the problem back to the Head Teacher and the Head Teacher gave the deputy a formal disciplinary warning.

If the member of staff becomes very defensive or aggressive, it is important for the line-manager to remain calm and avoid heightening the tension with blunt or incautious remarks. The line-manager should:

- maintain eye contact;
- keep body language open and relaxed; and
- remember, and remain focused on, the overall aims of the meeting.

If the initial concerns leading up to the discussions are unfounded, lesson observation will resolve the issue to the satisfaction of all concerned. If the concerns are well founded, the teacher is entitled to professional support and advice and the pupils are certainly entitled to effective teaching and learning. By the end of the meeting, the line-manager should have the beginning of some ideas about the support the teacher may need, and the teacher should be aware that the situation in which s/he is under-performing will not be allowed to continue.

The initial lesson observation

One or more lesson observations are necessary at this stage to form a clearer view of how and why things are going wrong in the classroom. It is preferable if observations take place with the teacher's 'worst' class or at the most difficult part of the day or week and without the teacher making special preparation for the observation. This is likely to 'capture' more of the reality of the learning experience in the classroom and lead to the production of an action plan for real improvement.

Senior leaders often find that their presence in the classroom has a distorting effect on pupils' behaviour. One way of minimising this effect is for the senior leader to make a number of short visits to the chosen class so that the pupils become more accustomed to the his/her presence. It is quite surprising how quickly pupils forget the presence of a visitor and, in reality, the observer is usually able to gain valuable information about what is, or is not, working in the classroom.

Training for lesson observation

There are different ways of observing a lesson. One way is to use an observation schedule like the one shown in Table 3.1 that directs attention towards different aspects of lesson structure and classroom management. It is also helpful to print Ofsted's judgement criteria on teaching and learning on the reverse of the schedule as a handy reference (see Table 2.1).

Those carrying out the lesson observation also need some training in the use of these approaches, as there is considerable scope for different interpretations of what is observed. Training should start with a discussion of what constitutes good teaching and learning using prompts such as the Ofsted criteria and the Professional Standards for Teachers.

It is then helpful for two observers to watch the same lesson using the same observation sheet and to compare notes and discuss any differences in interpretation. This will help to establish some common approaches and to take account of the subject or age differences of the pupils taught. Where line-managers are observing a key stage or a subject they are not familiar with, it is helpful for them to refer to the relevant National Curriculum documents before embarking on the observation.

However, in the initial lesson observation of an under-performing teacher, it may be better for the observer to avoid a prescriptive observation sheet and simply just write a description of what happens in the classroom. This open-ended approach helps to avoid the situation in which the observer approaches the lesson with preconceived ideas about what should or shouldn't be happening. It can present the teacher being observed with a non-judgemental account which may be a better starting point for initial self-reflection and follow-up discussion.

Table 3.1:   *Lesson observation sheet with prompts*

Date and time of observation	Name of teacher observed:_____
	Class observed:_____
	Name of observer:_____Room:_____
	No. of boys: _____ No. of girls:_____
	Judgement on lesson: ____
	1 = very good,
	2 = good,
	3 = satisfactory,
	4 = unsatisfactory
Start of lesson o Classroom routines o Lesson objectives o Links with previous learning o Starter activity	**Start of lesson commentary**
Main part of lesson o Variety of activities o Pace and challenge o Pupil response o Clarity/Structure of lesson o Quality of questioning o Management of behaviour issues o Relationships o SMSC* o Citizenship o ICT o Literacy o Numeracy o AFL** o Independent learning o Assessed books o Homework set o Use of LSA***	**Main part of lesson commentary**
End of lesson o Plenary o Reference back to lesson objectives o Classroom routines o Behaviour management	**End of lesson commentary**

*SMSC = Spiritual, Moral, Social and Cultural Education
**AFL = Assessment for Learning
***LSA = Learning Support Assistant

Point for reflection

Consider the following part lesson observation and identify two main areas for the teacher to reflect on.

Start of the lesson: The teacher was slightly late for the start of the lesson and then had to send a pupil to get the textbooks from another room. The pupils came into the room without any engagement with the teacher who was busily writing the lesson objectives on the board with his back to the door. He was also delayed by not having a board rubber and having to go next door to borrow one from another classroom. The lesson began in a slightly confused manner with the teacher giving out books and paper to pupils who did not have their exercise books and simultaneously talking at the pupils about what they had done last lesson.

After five minutes, the pupils – who were a lower ability Year 8 group – were given an apparently unrelated reading and written task to do. Calm briefly descended in the classroom until the pupils began shouting out to ask the teacher what the longer words in the text they had been given meant. The lesson topic was 'natural disasters'.

The follow-up discussion

At the end of the lesson, the observer should try to speak to the teacher briefly and encouragingly, however concerned the observer might be about the lesson just seen. The teacher observed may be feeling tense and anxious about the lesson observation and it is important to build on, and develop, any existing rapport. It is particularly important that the observer does not develop a judgemental approach here. Remember that the aim of the exercise is to encourage self-reflection and the self-confidence to try to improve. If the teacher feels s/he is being treated harshly or unduly critically, it can provoke or reinforce unhelpful defensive responses that may make further progress even more difficult.

The observer should arrange a mutually convenient time for the follow-up discussion and again care should be taken to have this discussion where it will not be interrupted, and to create a professional atmosphere. The observer should not allow the teacher to evade the discussion because s/he is 'too busy' or 'has another meeting'. It is quite possible that teachers who are having difficulties will be reluctant to face up to their situation since this lack of self-reflection and critical awareness is likely to be one of the reasons they are experiencing difficulties in the first place.

Setting targets

The line-manager doing the observation should ensure that the lesson observation is typed up and available to the teacher in the interview, but it is important for the observer to re-emphasise that s/he has deliberately carried out the observation in an unstructured way to avoid being judgemental. At this point it is helpful to encourage the teacher to 'talk through' the lesson observed from a personal point of view, identifying things s/he thought went well and other areas which could have been improved. However poor the lesson observed was, there will be some positives and it is important to focus on these first.

Point for reflection

Read the part lesson observations below and identify one positive in each which could be used as the starter for discussion with the teacher.

Case 1

Start of the lesson: Pupils came into the room in a reasonably orderly manner and the lesson objectives were already on the Overhead Projector (OHP). The teacher's command: 'look this way and listen in' produced a positive response from most of the class.

A lengthy (15-minute) explanation of the lesson followed and the teacher's voice level began rising over background chatter as pupils became restless. Sharp verbal interjections – 'right', 'so', 'OK' – were unsettling and not very effective at retaining the pupils' focus. Two boys at the back of the room were playing under the desks with their mobile phones unobserved by the teacher, who had begun reading a lengthy passage of text to the class.

Case 2

Start of the lesson: The class were waiting for some time outside the classroom as the teacher tidied the area after the previous class had left. The class were then greeted at the door and brought into the room in an orderly manner. Lesson objectives were displayed on the board. The register was taken while pupils were talking and one girl repeatedly tapped the teacher for attention. The teacher then shouted at the class for not paying attention to him/her.

In talking through the lesson, the observer should encourage the teacher to reflect on what went well and what s/he would have liked to change. Difficulties are likely to include either classroom management or curriculum and planning issues, and often both. Table 3.2 sets out some of the more common issues associated with curriculum and its planning, and behaviour management.

However, it is important at this stage not to focus on *all* of these at once. Generally, it is more helpful to begin with joint curriculum/planning issues

Table 3.2   *Common curriculum planning and behaviour management issues*

Common curriculum and planning issues	Common behaviour management issues
• A curriculum which has not been 'chunked' into manageable learning activities. • A restricted range of teaching and learning methodologies employed. • Poorly planned lessons lacking structure, variety and pace. • Lessons poorly adapted to the special needs of individual pupils within the group. • Inadequate resources, such as not enough textbooks for the class or poorly produced, badly photocopied worksheets. • Resources not properly matched to the needs and abilities of the pupils. • Poorly organised and deployed resources.	• Failure to establish or enforce consistent classroom standards. • Poor lesson openings (rushed, poorly prepared, too abrupt, too long). • Failure to establish adequate classroom routines or systems. • Talking over noise instead of dealing with it. • Ineffective shouting. • Poor classroom organisation. • Failure to maintain appropriate boundaries between teacher and pupil (allowing over-familiar or casual interactions in which the teacher–pupil boundary is (blurred). • Pleading with pupils to behave. • Arguing with a pupil. • Poor lesson endings (rushed, no time for reflection on what has been learnt).

since thorough preparation and good planning can avoid many behaviour management issues arising in the first place.

When the line-manager has done the lesson observation, it may be helpful to view the checklists above again, and to begin to see whether the teacher is passive, aggressive or assertive or the extent to which the teacher is moving between several approaches. Passive teachers who are inconsistent, lack routines and are overly reactive often switch, without any apparent warning to the pupils, into hostile teachers who use an angry tone of voice, fail to listen to pupils and can use sarcasm and insult. It can be a long, hard road to recovery for such teachers – and for their line-managers who will need persistence, optimism and considerable interpersonal skills to manage the situation.

Point for reflection

Read the following part lesson observation and decide where the teacher is passive, hostile or assertive.

The teacher arrived after the class had gone into the lesson and dropped the pile of papers she was carrying as she entered the room. Some of the pupils helped her pick them up but others jeered or made paper aeroplanes out of the papers. She thanked the pupils who helped her but made no other comment.

(Continued)   **39**

(Continued)

The teacher introduced the topic by referring to previous work that the pupils were adamant they had not yet done and began by asking them to complete this work. Some of the pupils opened their exercise books and pretended to work but others were openly defiant. Later it appeared that she had mixed up this group with another group she taught. She attempted to retrieve the situation by giving out some photocopies on a different topic (possibly intended for another group?) and when the pupils continued to be unresponsive she became angry and shouted at them for 'behaving like animals' and 'not knowing how to behave'. She loudly informed them that she had photocopied the work in colour especially for them because she knew she was going to have an observer in the lesson and they didn't deserve it.

The initial support plan

Having reviewed the lesson observation with the member of staff, the line-manager should try to agree no more than three areas for the teacher to work on, ensuring that one of these can easily be tackled so that success is built into the plan for the teacher. It is important for line-managers to be precise about the problems as they see them, evidencing their comments from the lesson description. An initial support plan will then need to be written with three SMART (Specific; Measurable; Achievable; Realistic; Time-lined) targets and a relatively short timescale for progress to be made. An example of a structure for such a plan is shown in Table 3.3.

Point for reflection

Read the following description of a lesson and decide what issues to focus on first in achieving improvement for this teacher.

Start of the lesson: The lesson began late because the pupils had to be collected and then moved to the computer room. As the pupils went up the corridor they were noisy and disturbed other lessons which had already started. In the computer room pupils were allowed to sit in friendship groups and the arrangement in the room meant that one group of boys were sitting facing each other but with their backs to the teacher (10 mins).

(Continued)

(Continued)

The lesson began with a lengthy description (15 mins) of how to access the website containing information for their research projects. The boys with their backs to the teacher began playing with their keyboards and chatting across to each other. The teacher raised his voice over the noise and then said generally, 'pay attention'. Once the pupils had made a start on the computer task (25 mins into lesson) the boys who had not been paying attention did not know how to access the website and one of them wandered across the room and started playing with the computer of another pupil, preventing him from working. The teacher told him to sit down and he did so reluctantly. Pupils began trying to print information from the website but the printer jammed (35 mins) and the teacher lost focus on classroom behaviour as he tried and failed to mend it. The technician was sent for and in the meantime the class began going onto other websites despite the teacher's general instruction to 'leave other websites alone, guys'. One pupil accessed a British National Front website.

End of the lesson: At the end of the lesson, only three pupils had got any information printed out from the website and this information was undergraduate-level material. The teacher's instruction 'pack up, guys' was hard to hear given the noise level in the room, and the lesson finished with no reflection on what had been learned. The class left the computer room as noisily as they had entered it and afterwards the technician discovered that the balls from three of the computer mice had been removed.

Table 3.3   *Support plan for an under-performing teacher*

Name of teacher: _____

Time period during which the plan will operate: _____

Name of line-manager: _____

Area for improvement	Time by which improvement should be shown	Resource implications (all if any)	Success criteria (how will we know when they have been achieved?)	How this plan will be monitored and evaluated
• Target 1				
• Target 2				
• Target 3				

Date on which plan will be reviewed:_____

For the teacher described above, the initial support plan shown in Table 3.4 may be appropriate. Apart from having one easy target, it is also helpful to set

Table 3.4 *Example of a completed support plan for an under-performing teacher*

Area for improvement	Time by which improvement should be shown	Resource implications (if any)	Success criteria (how will we know that it has been achieved?)	How this plan willbe monitored and evaluated
• **Target 1** Move seating in the computer room so that all pupils are facing the front and tell the pupils before the lesson that the lesson will start in the computer room (so that time is not wasted in collecting pupils).	Next lesson.	Caretaker time if assistance is needed to move chairs.	Pupils are all facing the front in the lesson.	The plan will be monitored through discussion between the line-manager and teacher and will be evaluated at the end of the support process in terms of its success in changing practice.
• **Target 2** Arrange for the ICT technician to check the equipment before you use the computer room (to avoid wasting time and losing focus in the lesson).	Next lesson.	ICT technician time.	Equipment functions.	
• **Target 3** Focus on a crisp start to the lesson, with all pupils listening to instructions, which must not take longer than 5 minutes and must be reinforced with board work or a handout which directs pupils to appropriate websites.	Next lesson.	Handouts.	Pupils listen to instructions and know what to do.	

one challenging target and one target which does not involve any personal adaptation by the individual, so that progress can be made and confidence built at the start of the process. It is important to ensure that the teacher understands that this is just the start of the process and that a number of different support plans which may be needed before the necessary standards are reached. Ensure that time targets are short so that a momentum for change can be established and follow up the plan with a further lesson observation where progress against the plan can be demonstrated.

The review meeting

Support plans should have short timescales and the review meeting is essential for reviewing progress and moving the teacher's practice forward. The line-manager should be positive and encouraging but also prepared to be firm with the teacher, not accepting inappropriate excuses for any inaction.

At this stage, it is not unusual for further difficulties to emerge in the teacher's practice and the line-manager can feel overwhelmed by the complexity of the task of restoring professional standards. However, the advice here is to remain focused, concentrating first on lesson planning, structure, pace and challenge and secondly on encouraging the teacher to use a wider variety of behaviour management techniques. In subsequent support plans, the following activities may help the teacher to improve his/her practice:

- Team teaching with a successful teacher.
- Joint lesson planning with the line-manager.
- Targeted observation of the teaching of excellent teachers (this is lesson observation with a series of prompts to focus the teacher's observation).
- Concentrating each week on a different behaviour management technique and aiming to use it in all lessons.
- Reading some relevant literature on modern behaviour management techniques and discussing this with the line-manager.
- Looking at video clips of good teaching and discussing them with the line-manager to identify what teachers are doing to help pupils to learn.
- Having a lesson filmed and discussing it with the line-manager.
- Attending relevant external in-service training.

All of this will take time, persistence and frequent lesson observations and reviews by the line-manager. There is no absolute time limit for improvement to be shown but the line-manager will soon get a sense of whether progress is actively being sought by the teacher. The successful completion of less challenging support plans will lead into more difficult areas where, hopefully, the professional relationship now established between the line-manager and the teacher will carry the process forward. The sense of satisfaction in seeing a colleague restore his/her professional standards and begin to function as at least a satisfactory teacher is considerable. The challenge then is to find ways of maintaining and developing this practice further.

When support is not enough

There are occasions when, despite the best efforts of the line-manager, the teacher fails to make the necessary progress. Often this is because the teacher cannot develop the skills of self-reflection and persists in not accepting that it is his/her practice which has to change. In this situation, the line-manager should carefully document the support given, the lack of progress and the teacher's response in review meetings. If, after several reasonable and manageable support plans, the teacher has shown no sign of attempting to improve, it will be important to make it clear to the teacher that the alternative to a successfully completed support plan may be competency/capability proceedings. If, after this warning and a further attempt to engage the teacher in making progress on a reasonable support plan, no change is evident, the line-manager must pass the issue and the records of what has been attempted so far over to senior management. Senior managers are likely to consult with the relevant teacher union to signal their intention to use established competency/capability proceedings.

Maintaining teacher performance through self-reflection

The aim of this chapter is to examine the role of self-reflection in improving teacher effectiveness, to prompt and extend self-reflection for teachers who are already self-reflective, and to provide assistance to line-managers who need to encourage self-reflection in teachers being supported to become effective.

The reflective teacher

Experience shows that it is the teacher's own performance, personal and professional skills, expectations and relationships in the classroom that are the key factors in influencing pupils' behaviour, attitudes and subsequent progress. When teachers possess the wisdom and resilience to adopt a reflective and objective view of their own practice, they also have the vital ingredients for enhancing their classroom practice.

This section takes a brief look at what it means to be reflective about one's professional practice. Louden (1991), for example, defines reflection as:

> *serious and sober thought at some distance from action . . . a mental process which takes place out of the stream of action, looking forward or (usually) back to actions that have taken place.*

There is a significant body of literature on *reflective practice* and, concomitantly, on the concept of the *teacher as a reflective practitioner*. According to Bloud, *et al.* (1985), reflection is part of the process of learning and is a generic term for those intellectual and effective activities in which individuals engage to explore their experiences in order to lead a new understanding and appreciation. Ross (1990) suggests that in teaching, reflection is 'a way of thinking about educational matters that involves the ability to make rational choices and to assume responsibility for those choices'. On the underlying principles of reflection, McKernan (1999) asserts that:

Perhaps the most outstanding feature of the professional is the capacity for self-evaluation and self-improvement through rigorous and systematic research and study of his or her own practice.

Similarly, Ross (1990) suggests that reflection is 'a way of thinking about educational matters that involves the ability to make rational choices and to assume responsibility for those choices'.

To be reflective is a disposition that can be acquired and its development can, and should, become a process that has both an individual and a whole-school perspective. Self-review, and the associated reflection on professional practice, is the fundamental principle that underpins the Ofsted Framework for Inspection (Ofsted, 2003c) and a teacher's professional and individual practice will be closely integrated into whole-school practice, development, monitoring and self-review.

Several factors may contribute to a judgement that a teacher is not performing to an expected standard in the classroom. These judgements are generally founded on hard data generated internally or externally, e.g. examination and test performance; internal monitoring systems. Collectively, they are likely to reveal a host of factors surrounding pupil performance and behaviours, as well as inhibitors to pupil progress.

For the individual member of staff who has the ability to be reflective and objective about how well the pupils appear to be learning, the indications of pupil/teacher under-performance may at first be vague, for example.

- increasingly unacceptable pupil behaviour at key points during the lesson;
- a feeling that it has taken considerable effort to get any work at all from some of the pupils; and
- feeling stressed and reacting to the situation by becoming more antagonistic towards those pupils perceived to be the main 'troublemakers'.

If no successful intervention occurs, then it is likely that the classroom climate will continue to deteriorate. In the worst cases, the breakdown of relationships between the teacher and some pupils can result in the display of overt, deliberate, challenging and provocative pupil behaviours. These classroom conditions make for an extremely unhappy existence for teachers and pupils alike and may have an adverse effect on every single member of the teaching group, producing much lower than predicted or acceptable pupil performances.

Many teachers will register their concern about deteriorating classroom experiences but in the case of teachers who lack the capacity to reflect on their experiences, this concern is often expressed in terms of blame directed towards pupils and/or school leaders and managers. Reflective teachers, on the other hand, will examine their own practice and performance, looking in detail at how their difficulties arose. They will then look for ways to improve the situation using their sources of professional support.

More confident teachers will understand the need to use different strategies, practise new skills, and to embed in daily practice an increasing range of effective teaching skills and behaviour management approaches. Less confident and less reflective teachers will need to build up and develop both the skills and the courage for self-reflection and the confidence and willingness to try new techniques and approaches. Line-managers will need to handle this situation sensitively, and several successive support plans may be necessary to begin to move an initially unreflective individual forward.

The reflective awareness model

Being reflective about our successes and areas needing development is a necessary precondition for learning to occur in order to improve our professional behaviours and practices. This state of reflective awareness can be expressed as a five-stage model – the 'conscious competence' learning matrix (see Figure 4.1). The model explains the process and stage of learning a new skill, behaviour, ability, techniques, etc. It is a useful reminder of the need to learn, and train others, in stages. Some claim the origins of the model go as far back as Confucius and Socrates with various modern interpretations and adaptations made since then. In essence, the stages of learning are expressed as being:

- Stage 1: unconscious incompetence
- Stage 2: conscious incompetence
- Stage 3: conscious competence
- Stage 4: unconscious competence
- Stage 5: conscious competence of unconscious competence.

The state of unconscious competence is where we do not know that we are not skilful or knowledgeable – we do not know that we do not know! A proportion of under-performing teachers will be at this stage and it is for middle and senior leaders in schools to help them identify and address these areas of under-performance if they are to become more effective. It is at this stage that some teachers will not recognise the need for learning – their confidence will exceed their ability.

When we become consciously incompetent, we realise that we would like to learn a skill, but are aware that our ability is limited – we know what we do not know. Learners (under-performing teachers) realise that by improving

iii	COMPETENCE	INCOMPETENCE	ii
CONSCIOUS	Teachers who achieve 'conscious competence' present little difficulty because they perform reliably at will. Even new skills can be acquired and performed with little or no assistance. The teacher will not reliably perform the skill unless thinking about it – the skill is not yet 'automatic' or 'second nature'. The teacher should be able to demonstrate the skill to another, but is unlikely to be able to teach it well to another person. Practice is the only effective way to progress.	These teachers are aware that they have gaps in their skills, knowledge and understanding. They are focused on filling these gaps using their own initiative or with the support of coaches and mentors. These teachers realise that by improving their skill or ability in this area, their effectiveness will improve. Ideally, they make a commitment to learn and practise the new skills and to move to the 'conscious competence' stage.	
UNCONSCIOUS	Teachers that fall into this category practise skills almost as second nature. The skills become so practised that they enter the unconscious parts of the brain – they become 'second nature'. It becomes possible for certain skills to be performed while doing other things. To avoid complacency, long-standing 'unconscious competence' needs to be checked periodically against new standards.	Teachers in this category pose the greatest challenge to school leaders. They have little or no awareness of the skill areas in which they have a particular deficiency. They might even deny the relevance or usefulness of the new skill. What is crucial here is that through effective support mechanisms, these teachers are helped to become conscious of their incompetence.	
iv	COMPETENCE	INCOMPETENCE	i

Figure 4.1   *The 'conscious competence' learning matrix*

their skills and abilities their effectiveness will improve. At this stage, it is not unusual to experience a drop in confidence as we practise the new skill as part of our learning and find that we do not always succeed. The implications for line-managers designing and offering a structured programme of support are clear: the teacher's practice may get worse before it gets better and the issue of the teacher's confidence will need careful handling.

When we become consciously competent we have acquired the new skill that can be performed reliably at will. We become more confident in our ability to be able to do it when we are consciously concentrating on what to do. We can do it if we know how. As learners we become more confident in our ability to be able to perform well when we focus on what to do. It is for middle and senior leaders to encourage and devise the support and ongoing monitoring in order to sustain the teacher's newly found proficiency. When the skills are blended together and embedded so that they become habits, we reach the stage of unconscious competence. Our confidence and abilities have peaked and we do not have to concentrate on what it is we have to do or know. We can do it, but might have difficulty in understanding and explaining how it is done.

The final stage of this learning model is when the learner (the teacher) has the ability to recognise deficiencies and develop skills in others, sometimes described as reflective consciousness. The need for middle and senior leaders to be able to operate at this level is essential for the identification and development of effective programmes of support for staff.

By having an understanding of our own learning processes we can begin to appreciate where we are in our own development of acquiring and using new skills. We must also appreciate that we all have different dispositions and find some new skills much easier to master than others, and that during the learning process we can find ourselves slipping into and out of the different stages depending on the skills involved. Practice is the key factor that determines our ability to progress, and with ever-increasing success comes fresh confidence.

Point for reflection

Using the conscious competence model, apply the following questions to each of the case studies presented below.

- What issue(s) needs to be addressed by school leaders?
- At what stage would you locate the teacher on the conscious competence continuum?
- What approach(es) might work best in the initial discussion with each teacher?
- What ongoing support and development opportunities might be appropriate in each case?

Case study 1

Sandra is a Business Studies teacher in a small secondary school. She teaches mainly Year 12 and Year 13 students, but does have a mixed-ability GCSE group. Over the time that Sandra has been at the school there has been a steady drop in the examination performance of the pupils in her GCSE groups.

The school is in an ex-mining community and she asserts, regularly and vocally, that her examination results are poor as a result of the pupils' poor attitudes towards learning and the lack of support she receives from the Senior Leadership Team (SLT).

(Continued)   **49**

(Continued)

The SLT, however, are concerned that they receive a significant number of requests for their support as part of the school's emergency response system, and that the reasons given for exiting a pupil are frequently minor.

When Sandra discusses the incident it is clear to the SLT that she does not understand or accept that the problem has been brought about by a number of contributory factors, and that she is capable of, and should be, planning to pre-empt and prevent the likelihood of them recurring. Sandra sees herself as a victim of 'poor management' and external factors that create pupils who do not come to school with aspirations and a desire to learn.

When the Senior Leader with responsibility for Teaching and Learning did a lesson observation and feedback of Sandra as part of the school's cycle, Sandra objected to some of the factually correct observations that had been made. She walked away from the senior member of staff and complained to the Head Teacher.

Despite the support the school has tried to give her to improve her practice and to develop new skills, Sandra is unable to see the benefits of trying to change and implement new practices. She continues to stand firm, maintaining that there is nothing wrong with her teaching – it is the pupils and the SLT that need to change.

Case study 2

Brian is an NQT in a middle-sized primary school in a town where there is a sizeable ethnic population. He is of a cheery disposition and eager to please and fit in with his colleagues. He started the year well, but as the first term drew on he began to feel that perhaps he had made the wrong choice of career.

He was feeling that his class were taking longer to respond to his directions and that it was becoming more difficult for him sustain the attention of the whole class. He had also become aware that over the period of time, some girls had not actually actively contributed in their lessons. Brian had started to doubt his own effectiveness.

Once he had identified what was the cause of his unease in meetings with the Deputy Head who was his mentor, an additional series of support strategies were put in place. By observing other colleagues, by discussing good practice, through working on his own skills in questioning techniques, Brian found an increasing confidence in his own abilities. He did successfully complete his NQT year, and has become more secure in his belief of his own capabilities.

(Continued)

Case study 3

Cath is a Maths teacher with three years' experience and works in a middle school. She successfully completed her NQT year at the same school. Although Cath had experienced some difficulties during her first year, the school has a good staff induction and ongoing support programme and she soon overcame the obstacles.

Her confidence has increased over the three years. She recognises that this is due to the extra support received from her colleagues and the practical benefits given her in being able to see a variety of approaches and practices elsewhere in the school. She has then had new ideas affecting her own approach and she possesses the enthusiasm to trial new methods for herself. As a result, Cath has developed her own distinctive style and has created a classroom environment where pupils are encouraged, motivated and taught the skills to enable them to become learners.

All of these developments have been made through consciously planning for, and putting into effect, strategies that produce positive outcomes. Cath is at a stage in her professional development where she knows that she will need to continue to plan thoroughly, reflect on each lesson and make amendments where necessary. She has come to appreciate, from her own learning experience, the parallels of her pupils' learning styles.

Case study 4

Diane is a teacher of 20 years' experience, and a Pastoral Head of Year in a large secondary school. She has always enjoyed the respect of her colleagues as her examination results are above the average in their value added, her classes are orderly, and her classroom has high quality pupils' work and interesting and relevant displays.

She is forthright in her views, but considerate of others' feelings. She has good relationships with her year group and pupils feel that she is 'sound' and listens to them. The parents that she liaises with hold her in high regard as they recognise that Diane does care and wishes to do her best for their child while at school.

A new Head Teacher came to the school, and Diane's skills and strengths soon became apparent to him. As part of restructuring the staffing of the school, the Head Teacher was of the opinion that Diane would be ideal in the role of Professional Tutor with the responsibility

---

(Continued)

(Continued)

for co-ordinating the Initial Teacher Training associates the school receives each year.

Diane was pleased to accept the position as she saw this as a rightful, if unexpected, promotion. She approached the role in an organised and meticulously planned manner, but what soon became apparent to her was that for 20 years she had been teaching successfully, but that this was based mainly on instinct and personality. When it came to delivering sessions to the student teachers, which would integrate the theoretical and the practical to aid their understanding of effectiveness in the classroom, Diane found that she did not necessarily possess the knowledge to do so.

Using a self-reflective approach

A key step for the reflective teacher and/or concerned line-manager to take is to maintain a clear perspective and to identify the nature of the problem. Preferably, the problem should be pinpointed in its early stages, as this is when intervention is likely to be more easily introduced and effective in achieving results. The following questions may serve to enable teachers and line-managers to make an initial identification of the issues and, through discussion, assess where on the conscious competence model the teacher is and to plan accordingly.

Point for reflection

Consider your own teaching in relation to the following questions.

Questions for reflection	Response
What is my main concern?	
Is the cause of my concern demonstrated across more than one teaching group in the same year group?	
Is the cause of my concern occurring across a number of year groups?	
Is it one particular pupil who is causing the concern?	

(Continued)

(Continued)

Is it a small group of pupils causing the concern?	
Is the scheme of work new, or changed in some respect?	
Have I adapted the work to the ability of the group(s) taught?	
Am I aware of the special needs of individuals in the group(s) and have I adapted the work accordingly?	
Have I planned the lesson thoroughly with a starter, a variety of activities taking account of different learning styles, and a plenary to reinforce learning?	
Has the working environment changed?	
Do aspects of the working environment present difficulties for my teaching?	
Have I asked for support from my line-manager to resolve any concerns?	

The answers to these first tentative questions may, in themselves, provide a clearer, more objective view of recent events. They cover three main areas for further investigation, although, in practice, under-performing teachers often have difficulties in all areas simultaneously:

- Effective teacher management of pupil behaviour.
- Planning for effective teaching and learning.
- The physical environment for effective teaching and learning.

In helping teachers to think about their own behaviour and in order to improve and extend their skills in managing pupil behaviour, it is important to emphasise that:

Behaviour can be changed. Behaviour is not totally static and fixed. Students can learn new and different ways of relating, responding and coping in social settings, with their formal schooling and with situations of conflict. They can also learn from the kind of discipline we exercise and the modelling we offer as teachers.

(Rogers, B., 2003)   **53**

Teachers therefore need to be fully aware that their personal and professional behaviour in the classroom has a significant effect on the behaviour of the pupils. They need to consider carefully the perceptions pupils will have of their behaviour, be conscious of the unspoken messages of body language, and give full attention to the language they use in the classroom and the importance of maintaining a positive approach.

Teacher behaviour: pupils' perceptions

The importance of strong professional relationships between staff and pupils cannot be underestimated. It is an absolute necessity that the relationships in the classroom should be seen by pupils to be without favour to the few, and fair and consistent towards all. Relationships will stem from the active and consciously planned elements the teacher brings into the classroom, and those things that are usually unplanned, instinctive and individual responses to human interactions. It is clearly much easier to identify the tangible factors, less so those aspects that are not so readily defined and subject to a pupil's perception. Hay/McBer (2000) found that pupils perceived effective teachers to be those who demonstrate that they care about and value individuals. These teachers:

- have a belief in the ability of the pupils;
- have high expectations and realistic ambitions for pupils;
- treat pupils with respect;
- know pupils as individuals;
- involve pupils in planning and decision making;
- emphasise the positive in pupils;
- give clear directives;
- take responsibility for misunderstandings in teacher/pupil interactions;
- avoid labelling and jumping to conclusions;
- listen to pupils;
- provide personal support where appropriate;
- care for the classroom environment; and
- are genuine.

Reflective teachers may well ponder how they demonstrate each of the above, and then consider in what light they believe their own pupils see those characteristics in them. In view of the possibility that the teacher's views may be at variance with the pupils' perceptions, it is worth taking time to identify how you believe you show these qualities to your classes.

- Would the pupils' answers be different for different classes?
- Would pupils in the same teaching group probably give different responses to some, or all, of the points?
- If so, what can you do to ensure consistency and equity towards all pupils?
- Can you identify what it is that causes you to respond differently to some pupils?

Ascertaining the views and perceptions pupils have of their teachers can be discovered by using a questionnaire based on research into teacher effectiveness carried out by Hay/McBer (2000). The anonymous questionnaire, which can be administered by the teacher or a colleague, can be given to all pupils or to a representative sample. Answers to the questions will reveal specific areas of teachers' interactions and relationships in the classroom and the pupils' interpretations! Having the pupils' views will enable the reflective teacher to assess their area(s) of development and then to consider the precise action and support required to address the issues.

Point for reflection

The following is an example of a pupil perception questionnaire which you might wish to use with some of your pupils.

Which words do you think best describe your teacher?	Yes	No	Unsure
Kind			
Listens to me			
Encourages me			
Has faith in me			
Likes teaching children			
Likes teaching their subject			
Takes time to explain things			
Helps me when I am stuck			
Tells me how I am doing			
Allows me to have my say			
Cares for my opinion			
Makes me feel clever			
Treats people equally			
Stands up for me			
Makes allowances			
Tells the truth			
Is forgiving			

What has become clear over time is the necessity for teachers to employ techniques that are rooted in the positively framed and non-confrontational methodology. Pupils need to be considered as individuals, with varying personal, social, emotional and educational needs. If these needs are not met, then teachers are more likely to encounter the pupil who is not afraid to challenge when feeling affronted, excluded or disregarded.

However, it is perfectly possible for the reflective teacher to view him or herself as possessing certain traits and characteristics, but for this perception not to be shared by the pupils. This sometimes occurs when the teacher believes that s/he holds and demonstrates certain attitudes and values, but through the pressures of time, pupil numbers, delivering the subject content, or managing particular pupils it can be very easy to not actually exhibit these qualities to the class.

Point for reflection

In reaching the conclusion that teaching is more than just the delivery of the curriculum, we need to consider the following questions in relation to pupil behaviour.

- What are the school's values and principles? How do I promote and convey these in my teaching?
- Do I actively plan for and teach my pupils the behaviours for learning?
- What words, attitudes and actions do my pupils see me display most frequently?
- Do I have clear and known routines in my lessons?
- Do I model the same behaviours as I wish pupils to display?
- How do I reward and praise all pupils for their work and their behaviour?
- Am I consistent and fair in giving praise and rewards?
- Do pupils value and respond positively to the praise and rewards I use?
- How and when do I apply sanctions?
- Am I consistent and fair in applying sanctions?
- Do the sanctions I use modify the pupils' behaviour effectively?
- What do I do to create a positive and welcoming environment in my classroom?
- How do I ensure that each pupil feels I know him or her individually, and care about his or her progress?

Teacher behaviour: using influential body language

There are vital messages that we all convey, and receive, at a subconscious level, by our body language. These messages and our reactions are instinctive and very powerful. We all know that feeling of being sure we can sum somebody's personality up within a very short time of meeting them for the first time. We believe we can identify essential messages from the way they present themselves. Over 65 per cent of communication is done non-verbally. Our postures, movements and gestures convey a huge amount of information about our interpersonal attitudes.

> When problems do arise, the ability to exercise authority convincingly requires personal qualities such as confidence, assertiveness and decisiveness. These are attitudes that are easily recognised but much more difficult to describe as there are subtleties in the communication which are crucial and can easily be overlooked when attempting to convey these impressions.
>
> (Robertson, 2002)

So we can see that if we are aware of how we present to others, we can in fact learn to use positive gestures to communicate with others and to eliminate gestures that may give negative signals. This can make it more comfortable to be with people and make you more acceptable and approachable to them.

Reflective teachers should consider the way in which they present themselves to pupils, including their non-verbal behaviour, their general appearance and the way in which things are said. The characteristics found in effective teachers are:

- a professional but relaxed appearance;
- the use of exaggerated facial expressions, e.g. a gaze or raised eyebrows;
- confident and relaxed non-verbal behaviours, e.g. relaxed shoulders, resting on one leg, sitting down when a pupil is standing, hands loose – not clenched;
- illustrative gestures to show how the class should respond;
- kneeling or getting down to the level of the child;
- controlling gestures;
- smiling face;
- self-pointing gestures;
- calm and relaxed quality of voice for the majority of the time; and
- resistance to pupil-instigated interruptions.

In the classroom, it is the teacher's high expectations of his/her pupils and their work, the teacher's ability to model the behaviours and attitudes we wish to see in pupils and the establishment of strong supportive relationships between the teacher and the pupils that are our most effective tools. Our body language will convey all of these factors, and for this reason reflective teachers should try to be objective about their own habits and patterns, and to take time observing the body language, gestures and reactions of others in a variety of social groupings. This is not only entertaining, but will also help to develop one's awareness of our most fundamental means of communication!

Teacher behaviour: the body language of teaching styles

The body language we use is a reflection of the teaching style, attitudes and relationships that the teacher conveys in the classroom. Body language is a vital component in how we communicate and in how pupils interpret the teacher's intentions and emotional outlook. Research has shown that the two important factors in effectiveness are the teacher's ability to motivate pupils by enthusiasm, friendliness and helpfulness, and the ability to deal with confrontation. There are some fundamental behaviours that we subconsciously display which can be regarded as clear signs to pupils about how the teacher regards them, whether they are positive or more negative in appearance. Typically teachers' behaviours fall predominantly into one of three main teaching styles:

- passive;
- hostile; or
- assertive.

Correspondingly, there are typical behaviours that accompany these three traits. If we describe in general terms how staff behave at the extreme end of these characteristics, it will help reflective teachers to identify the positive traits they already possess, and to avoid adopting, or maintaining, the less helpful, or negative subconscious attitudes in the drive to maximise their potential as effective practitioners. Body language is under the direct effect of the attitudes and beliefs that the teacher holds and displays in the classroom.

The 'passive' teacher's body language
Passive teachers are ineffective because they may do some or all of the following:

- ignore inappropriate behaviour;
- react inconsistently;
- threaten or plead;
- give up;
- lack routine;
- have poor organisational skills; and
- react to poor behaviours.

This can lead pupils to feel confused as the boundaries keep changing and to learn that teacher attention can be gained through misbehaviour. As seeking any sort attention is a goal for some pupils, clearly this is a very negative way for any such pupils to have their particular needs met. The body language and gestures that indicate this teaching style can include:

- a preference to stay behind the desk and reluctance to move around the room;
- few or no words of welcome as pupils arrive in the room;
- looking flustered and continuing with the lesson through pupil noise;
- nervous hand movements that may be 'fiddling' with watch, rings, buttons, loose change;
- arms folded as a defensive gesture;
- head and eyes looking downwards;
- ignoring unacceptable behaviour; and
- ignoring inappropriate/insufficient work.

The 'hostile' teacher's body language

The hostile teacher is ineffective because the attitudes displayed can be seen by pupils as being either confrontational and challenging, or intimidating and bullying. For some pupils it is as though the gauntlet has been thrown down, and they feel compelled to respond; others would prefer to adopt a low profile and not engage with the lesson or the teacher, just being passive so as not to attract the hostile teacher's attention. The features of this style of teacher can be:

- an angry, aggressive tone of voice;
- an inability to listen to the pupil;
- inconsistent and unfair reactions;
- use of sarcasm and insult;
- an expectation that pupils will misbehave;
- overreacting when pupils do misbehave; and
- a tendency to label pupils.

It is not surprising that students do not feel valued or welcome when they encounter a 'hostile' teacher. The pupils can, in turn, become angry and confrontational. This will have a detrimental effect on the attitudes and the ability to learn in the pupils directly involved in any confrontation, and the other members of the class will also become adversely affected, as the negative atmosphere that is generated generally discourages a positive attitude to learning. The body language of the hostile teacher can include:

- a loud and aggressive, sometimes accusing tone of voice;
- body becoming rigid;
- foot or finger tapping, showing irritation or impatience;

- intimidating gestures such as leaning over a pupil or jabbing the air;
- hands on hips;
- brusque movements and speech;
- equipment/resources being held and used as a 'weapon';
- invasion of pupils' personal space; and
- 'put-downs' and belittling of pupils' efforts.

The 'assertive' teacher's body language

Assertive teachers are usually effective teachers. These teachers demonstrate that they care for the pupils, themselves and the environment by:

- having positive expectations of the pupils;
- having positive expectations and confidence in their own ability to manage the classroom;
- establishing clear boundaries and routines;
- being consistent and fair;
- knowing the pupils as individuals;
- listening to the pupils and valuing their opinions;
- creating opportunities for pupils to engage with their learning physically, intellectually and emotionally; and
- modelling behaviour for learning.

The body language displayed by the effective teacher is one that exudes a confidence in both the teacher's abilities and expectations, and a confidence that the pupils will also display positive attitudes towards their learning and participation in the lesson. Assertive practitioners are often found to:

- greet pupils upon entering the room;
- give clear and specific directions;
- issue reminders about classroom rules when appropriate and in a low-key manner;
- use techniques in pre-empting and de-escalating poor pupil behaviour;
- circulate among all pupils in the room;
- use humour – but always *with* and never *at* pupils;
- maintain confident, upright body positions;
- have an ability to make, and hold, strong eye contact;
- physically stoop to the pupil's level, when appropriate, for effective communication;
- use open arm and hand gestures;
- give non-verbal gestures as signs to the pupils;
- allow pupils time to think and then respond to questions, without being afraid of the 'space' this requires;
- listen to pupils, valuing their contributions; and
- stay alert and aware of pupils' behaviour and work at all times.

Teacher behaviour: interaction zones

Like other animals, man has his own portable 'air bubble' that he carries around with him and its size is dependent on the density of the population in the place where he grew up. The personal zone distance is therefore culturally determined.

(Pease, 1990)

There are four zone distances in which interactions happen. It is as well to be aware of these and to avoid inadvertently straying into a zone than can cause a pupil to feel uncomfortable, as this can frequently cause an undesirable reaction in a child who is already suffering from poor social skills, poor self-esteem or is of a volatile nature caused by external factors. The zones are:

- Intimate zone: 15–46 cm
- Personal zone: 46 cm–1.2 m
- Social zone: 1.2–3.6 m
- Public zone: over 3.6 m.

Being aware of the zones (described in Table 4.1) helps the teacher to appreciate how pupils may sometimes react to 'their space' being invaded.

Table 4.1 *Zones of interaction (adapted from Pease, 1990)*

Intimate zone	It is the intimate zone that is the most important one to be aware of the implications for. This is the zone that is regarded as only to be entered into by those who are emotionally close to that person. It is easy to see why some pupils find it intolerable to be placed in a situation with a member of staff at such close proximity, in reaction to some inappropriate classroom incident. The very nature of the teacher's response by taking this action is likely to be interpreted by the pupil as confrontational and unjustified.
Personal zone	The personal zone is the distance that we stand from one another at social events and friendly gatherings. As classroom space is limited, pupils and teachers automatically find themselves frequently operating within this zone. So to enter a pupil's personal space requires that there will be positive relationships and a positive climate in the classroom in order to be able to function in a friendly and supportive manner.
Social zone	The social zone is the distance we stand from strangers and people we do not know very well.
Public zone	The public zone is the distance we choose to stand at in which we feel most comfortable talking to a large group of people.

Point for reflection

As a reflective teacher, you may find it an interesting exercise to keep a log over two days that describes the pupils' behaviour, and your response to incidents. As objectively as possible, judge whether your style was assertive, passive or hostile. Consider how this conscious appraisal of your behaviour and reactions might influence your future practice and professional development needs.

	Student Behaviour	Teacher Response	Assertive? Hostile? Passive?
Day 1			
Day 2			

Behaviour log

Teacher behaviour: using influential speech

Influential speech is another element of an effective teacher's performance in the classroom. It is both an art and a science at the same time! The presentation, choice of vocabulary, modulation of the voice, use of pauses and audience eye contact, are all factors identified in the highly refined and researched area of successful sales and political manipulation, and the same principles can be applied back in the classroom!

> An understanding of the subtleties of language and the way in which the brain processes it should be part of every teacher's repertoire. It is a simple truth that everything we say will have an influence over children in our classrooms.

(Vass, 2002)

How we phrase our instructions can improve the likelihood of the pupils' compliance. How we address our audience will influence their response to us. This is not revolutionary, but it will be effective! Simply replacing a 'please' with a 'thank you' at the end of a request will improve the chances of pupil compliance immediately. This simple strategy is effective because the tone of the request changes. The teacher is now implicitly expecting the pupil's compliance through the use of the word 'thanks'. 'Please' does not place the same expectation on the pupil. The adoption of the 'broken record' technique and repeating a request three times is also likely to produce a positive outcome. This works in most instances, as it would be a very determined pupil who would be able to withstand the subtle workings of 'the rule of three'. But as with other patterns of behaviour, reflective teachers will, at first, have to consciously plan to rephrase what they would normally find themselves saying. Eventually this conscious competence will become unconscious competence and the new behaviour is learned and embedded and reflective teachers can extend their own repertoire of new behaviours and strategies in the classroom.

Other behaviour management techniques promoted by professionals who work in related areas of pupil behaviour also testify to the efficacy of applying learned responses both to pre-empt pupil behaviour and to respond to situations. The following approaches demand that the practitioner adopts a consciously planned approach to intervening and supporting good pupil behaviour through the use of influential vocabulary. We need to move away from the more human trait of automatic, instinctive, unthinking responses that can cause the pupil and teacher alike to be caught in a negative, downward spiral. The skills and strategies that are proven to be influential are:

- *Pause direction,* e.g. 'Name, pause . . . back to work thanks'. This gains the student's attention before the instruction is given.
- *Privately understood signals.* The use of a sign or gesture that is understood by all pupils, or possibly an individual pupil.
- *Proximity praise.* The teacher notices a pupil who is not carrying out actions as directed; the teacher will then praise and describe the desired behaviour to pupils nearby who are carrying out the instruction as requested.
- *Physical proximity.* The teacher notices a pupil who is not on task. By moving towards them, pupils will often be refocused on the task without any verbal redirection.
- *Tactical ignoring.* The teacher focuses on the pupils who are behaving appropriately. Tactical ignoring can also be useful for ignoring 'secondary' behaviours so that the teacher can stay focused on the main issue.
- *Distraction and diversion.* The use of humour, or asking the student a question, calling a student over to have a quiet word, not as a reprimand, but work-related.
- *Partial agreement.* If the pupil challenges the teacher, the teacher can agree in part to the challenge, but then redirect the pupil back to the work, e.g. 'Matthew may have kicked your chair, but I need you to open your book at page 34'.
- *Using 'I' statements.* Use the 'I' statement to reinforce how you feel about the behaviour, not about the individual person.
- *'When . . . then' directions, e.g.* 'When you have done this . . . then you can do that'. This will allow the pupil to feel some control.
- *Question and feedback.* It is best to focus on what the pupils should be doing: 'What should you be doing?' gives the focus, unlike 'What are you doing?'

- *Rule reminders.* Give directions or correction by a reminder of the class rules.
- *Use positive repetition to get students on task.* Give directions, look for students following the directions. Say the name, repeat the direction, and make a positive comment.
- *Take up time.* Give the pupil enough time to do what has been asked by making the request, then moving away while the request is complied with. It will avoid unnecessary confrontation, and set the expectation that the pupil will conform.
- *Choice direction.* If the pupil continues not to conform, the teacher offers a series of choices about the consequences of making an 'unwise' choice. The consequence must be clear and enforceable.
- *Re-establishing a working relationship with the pupil.* It is important to signal to the student that the working relationship is continuing despite the difficulties.

In all of this, interventions to curb unwanted pupil behaviours should be kept as low-key as possible. The focus should always be on the learning that is going on in the classroom. Dealing with any inappropriate behaviour that causes this to be disrupted for other pupils is unnecessary, and can even be 'rewarding' for the pupil at the centre of it, who may well be enjoying the attention.

Point for reflection

Reflecting on your own practice, consider the interventions you use and at what point in any incident you respond with their use. It may be revealing for you to keep a log of the range of interventions you use over a period of days, or with a particular class, noting:

- their frequency;
- whether learning was disturbed; and
- how effective the strategy was.

Reflect on alternative strategies as shown below. Could other less intrusive strategies have worked?

Non-verbal messages	The 'look' or gesture that will refocus the pupil's attention.	Least intrusive
Tactical or planned ignoring	On occasions it is pragmatic not to interrupt the learning of others at a particular point, and to follow up any inappropriate behaviour at another point later in the lesson.	⬆

(Continued)

(Continued)

Description of reality	Stating clearly what the pupil is doing. This is often reminder enough to focus the pupil on what s/he should be doing.		
Simple direction	A description of what the pupil has been asked to do.		
Rule reminder	Draw the pupils' attention to the known and expected code of behaviour.		
Question and feedback	Noticing inattentive behaviour the teacher may then question the pupil and expect the pupil to articulate the reply when asked what the desirable behaviour should be.		
The 'stuck record', blocking or assertive statement	The teacher repeats the instruction three times.		
Choice and consequence	The teacher states the desirable behaviour and points out to the pupil that s/he has a choice: to make the right choice and comply, or to make the wrong choice and have a consequence attached to that inappropriate choice.		
Exit procedure	The exclusion of a pupil should only be used in extreme cases where the well-being and safety of others is called into question. The teacher should make certain s/he understands the school's policy and processes when such action is deemed necessary.	**Most intrusive**	

Robertson (2002) summarises the general principles for interventions in the following ways:

- Whenever possible, err on the side of low-key interventions that present co-operative relationships with students.
- Show regard for students or, at the very least, respect.

- Try to keep interventions as private as possible.
- Try to remain calm and avoid unhelpful feelings.
- Always follow up on any unresolved problem.
- Defer dealing with situations that are likely to encroach on your teaching time.
- Try to improve your relationships with students or, at least, not worsen them.

Teacher behaviour: being positive

The key principle to which the effective teacher must subscribe is to phrase every behaviour expectation, and every praise of good behaviours observed, in a positive way. Through the stating in positive terms of what it is the pupils are to undertake, the teacher will be explicit, offering more chances of pupils knowing exactly what is required of them. Teachers sometimes have a tendency to preface instructions with a negative, e.g. 'Don't push. Don't talk. Don't take so long to settle down'. Much more effective and helpful to pupils and the creation of a positive learning environment is to describe the desired behaviour in giving the instruction, e.g. 'Remember our rule to line up quietly, in an orderly manner; As soon as you sit down I want to see you take out your equipment, then sit facing me, giving me your full attention.' In the same way, behaviours that conform to the teacher's expectations must be praised and rewarded, thus increasing the likelihood of the pupils replicating those same behaviours. e.g. 'Thank you for all being so punctual to the lesson.' 'Sarah, you have presented this work following the precise format we described in class. Well done.'

Using praise

What is the easiest way to motivate students? Praise. The most effective? Praise. What positive recognition can you give to your students at any time? Under all circumstances? Praise.

(Canter and Canter, 1992)

Praise is a vitally important aspect of the effective teacher's repertoire. It is the one part of the teacher's armoury that can help influence and modify pupil behaviour. The sanctions and consequences given to unwanted behaviours serve only to limit the behaviours. In recognising the truth of this, we can begin to design the offering of praise and rewards so that they become purposeful, successful strategies.

First, let us consider the nature of praise and rewards for pupils. Praise can be verbal and non-verbal but it will only be well received if valued by the pupils. Reflective teachers should carefully consider the type of praise they offer, the occasions upon which praise is earned, and the frequency with which praise is earned. To be effective, praise needs to fulfil the following criteria:

- Pupils must feel that it is personal to them.
- Pupils must believe the praise is genuine and earned.
- The praise/reward must be appropriate.
- Praise should be specific and describe the positive reason for which it is being given.
- The teacher must be consistent in awarding praise.
- The teacher must be fair in awarding praise.
- The teacher must use praise regularly and in a ratio of at least 5:1.

Additionally, in order to maximise its effectiveness with pupils in classrooms, praise should also:

- be natural and warm;
- be varied and imaginative;
- get their attention; and
- be accompanied by good eye contact.

The effective deployment of praise can help the teacher to:

- reinforce positive expectations of behaviour and work;
- motivate pupils to repeat the positive behaviour associated with the praise;
- give individual pupils affirmation and raise their confidence;
- create a positive learning environment where effort and challenge is rewarded;
- create and sustain positive relationships with pupils; and
- allow pupils to achieve their potential.

As adults we are pleased to receive praise for our efforts, and if we believe those efforts have gone unnoticed and unacknowledged, we are swift to feel aggrieved and unappreciated. When praised, we can bask in the warm after-glow for some considerable time! If praise can mean so much to us, then we can begin to grasp how powerful praise can be when used as a means of influencing pupils' behaviour.

In conclusion, teachers need to focus clearly on their own behaviour in the classroom if they wish to prompt good behaviour from their pupils. They need to think about creating positive, assertive body language, operating in an appropriate interaction zone and using influential language which can contribute to a positive climate in the classroom.

Planning for effective teaching and learning

In this subsection, we examine some of the main factors that contribute to good planning for teaching and learning and encourage teachers to reflect on their current practice. There is a wealth of material available to all staff in schools that focuses on pedagogy and effective practice in teaching, e.g.

national strategies materials. It is important that reflective teachers consider some very fundamental questions regarding the nature of their own teaching.

Point for reflection

A basic set of questions, to help teachers become reflective about their practice, is set out below. It is important to answer them positively, possibly as a self-review exercise or as a preparation for a performance review with your team leader.

- Are all my lessons planned and designed to meet the social and emotional needs of all pupils?
- Am I cognisant of the pupils who have Individual Education Plans (IEPs), and do I plan accordingly?
- Do I have sufficient information about my pupils' prior attainment and knowledge, and plan the lesson accordingly?
- Are the learning objectives the focus of the lesson that drives the structure of the activities of the teacher and the pupils?
- Are the learning objectives, and the means by which they will be achieved, shared with the pupils?
- Do I know the preferred learning style of each pupil?
- Do I take appropriate steps to ensure that lessons offer variety in their approach to ways of learning?
- Do my lessons have appropriate pace and opportunities for pupils to interact with their learning?
- Do I plan well for the application of the teaching skills of questioning, explaining and modelling?

If these factors are not planned for and delivered in the most effective manner, then it is clearly going to adversely affect pupils' learning in that particular lesson. Lessons should be designed and structured so that:

- they are part of a sequence of lessons, and pupils know where the lesson sits within the whole;
- the content of the lesson takes into account pupils' prior knowledge and attainment, as well as preferred learning styles;
- the learning objectives are made explicit to pupils;
- the body of the lesson is devised into sections/parts/episodes, each of which will act as a step towards the next;
- each lesson ends with a plenary that reviews the learning and allows the teacher to gauge success in fulfilling the learning objectives. The pupils' responses will then inform the teacher's planning and delivery of subsequent lessons.

If the reflective teacher is planning well and according to pupils' needs, and pupils find the lessons engaging and participatory, then the foundation for pupil progress is firmly in place.

Point for reflection

Pupils' learning will best occur when certain conditions and factors are present. The reflective teacher might find it useful to see how a sample of his/her lesson plans reflects the criteria for learning.

Components of how we learn best

Features	Yes	Partially	No
Challenge in learning objectives			
Support available			
Relevance clear			
Structured			
Short-term goals/targets			
Active participation			
Variety			
Needs identified			
Feedback given			
Achievement			

Teachers who are struggling should always do detailed lesson plans and should evaluate the success of the plan at the end of the lesson. If the school does not have a model lesson plan layout used by all teachers, the example in Table 4.2 could be used.

Apart from careful lesson planning, thought must be given to how the teacher conveys his/her expectations of high standards of behaviour, effort and the presentation of work in order to achieve high quality work. Clearly identifying and articulating what those expectations are, then breaking them down into component parts, will enable the teacher to identify what s/he needs to teach the pupils. In this way the teacher is able to clearly and precisely express those expectations to the pupils and to reinforce them in the interactions that occur within the classroom. The answers to the questions below will allow effective teachers to

Table 4.2   *Example of a lesson planning proforma*

Lesson plan

Teacher_____ Class_____ Levels/Grades_____
Date_____ Room_____ Subject/Topic_____

Lesson objectives: *(What do you want all of the pupils to have learned by the end of this lesson?)*

More able: *(What additional learning have you planned for the most able members of the group?)*

SEN: *(Refer to any IEPs/IBPs for members of the group)*

Activity	Time: one 50-minute lesson
Starter activity which connects lesson with previous learning of pupils.	5 mins
Brief explanation of lesson objectives, connecting them with prior learning together with an outline of what will be happening in the lesson with timescales.	5 mins
Activity 1– an activity which relates to one style of learning e.g. literary, visual, kinaesthetic.	15 mins
Activity 2 – an activity which relates to a different style of learning.	15 mins
Plenary – an activity which reinforces the learning in the lesson.	10 mins

teach their precise expectations to their pupils. Too often teachers may believe that pupils 'should know' what is expected, and consequently fail to teach it to the students. It is important to realise that teachers' expectations need to be taught, modelled by themselves, and the pupils reminded regularly. It is not realistic for teachers to think that because they taught the class something once, all pupils should remember and act upon it. Teachers need to constantly state their expectations and praise pupils when the expectations are met. In this way, pupils are more likely to hear the message and modify their actions accordingly.

Point for reflection

Use the following questions to help you reflect on the ways in which you convey your expectations of high standards of presentation and conduct.

What are my expectations of pupils?	
What equipment do I want pupils to bring to each lesson?	
How do I want pupils to be seated at the start of the lesson?	
How do I want pupils to work in pairs/groups?	

(Continued)

(Continued)

What signal shall I use to inform pupils that they should commence/end an activity?	
How do I want pupils to present their written work?	
What is an acceptable noise level for different activities?	
How do I expect pupils to contribute to plenaries?	
At what point in the lesson do I give pupils homework, and how is it recorded?	
When do I expect homework to be handed in and how will this be organised?	

Point for reflection

Consider what expectations the teacher described below has created in his classroom and the extent to which the lesson was planned to meet the needs of the pupils.

The teacher was late to the lesson as were half a dozen pupils who drifted in over a period of ten minutes. The latecomers neither offered nor were asked to explain their lateness and the teacher made no comment on his own lateness. Lesson objectives were written on the board but not referred to until half-way through the lesson. The first activity was to read a lengthy passage from the textbook but two of the pupils with special educational needs (SEN) clearly struggled to do this despite the help of an LSA who was not given a lesson plan and had to guess what the lesson was about. The second activity was to answer questions on the passage, writing the answers in exercise books. Several pupils called out that they did not have exercise books and were given paper. Pupils were then left to work through the questions with the teacher moving round the room trying to keep pupils on task. Pupils began to chat and go off task as soon as the teacher was dealing with an individual pupil. At the end of the lesson which finished when the bell went and the pupils got up and left the room, some pupils had written nothing; others had written one-word answers despite being asked to 'write in detail'. The pupils working on paper left the papers behind as they left the room and the teacher, rushing to collect in the textbooks, made no attempt to pick them up.

The physical environment for effective teaching and learning

Planning for the best possible conditions in order to engage pupils will also require teachers to optimise the physical environment. In doing so teachers will be expressing, implicitly, the values and expectations they hold in relation to pupil behaviour and the worth of the subject being taught. As always, teachers must be models of the behaviours and attitudes they wish to instil in pupils, so the way in which the teacher organises the classroom, sets out and uses the resources in it, keeps it in a good state of repair, etc. sends out a strong message to pupils.

A major consideration for the reflective teacher is how to set out the furniture to best effect. Some teachers have a tendency to organise their teaching space formally, e.g. straight rows of desks with pupils facing the front of the class. While this layout may offer a form of security for the teacher, it does not necessarily offer the pupils a lively, more participatory style of engagement with their learning. If the goal of education is to develop learners, then we must be flexible in our thinking and planning and use all of the available resources in a creative, effective and safe manner.

For some teaching rooms and teaching groups, the furniture is more readily adaptable if desks are grouped together, or arranged in a horseshoe with a centre panel of desks. Whichever pattern is adopted it should lend itself to a variety of pupil groupings and working methods that cause the minimum of disruption. An arrangement of desks where pupils simply turn their chairs in order to form a group to facilitate group work, or where a minimum number of desks need to be moved to create an open floor space is the ideal. Clearly, whatever the layout adopted, it is essential that all pupils are able to see and hear the teacher and have access to any other vital equipment in the room. Having decided on the best layout of the furniture, it is then essential for the smooth running of the class that the teacher devises a seating plan for all the classes that use the room. This will allow the teacher to plan desirable pupil groupings in order to maximise positive outcomes.

The physical environment will also reflect the routines and expectations the teacher has for his/her pupils. For example, the effective teacher will plan for and organise the room to facilitate the orderly entrance of pupils and the placement of their belongings in a specific area or storage space. Equipment, too, should be stored, issued, used and collected by pupils, following the modelling of the teacher, with the same clear and shared knowledge of how to use it properly and with respect.

Wall displays

The physical environment is enhanced by interesting and focused wall displays. These should be informative and help pupils to understand what it is they need to know, incorporating keywords central to the areas of study. Wall displays are also dramatic ways of celebrating and promoting achievement when displaying pupils' work. Pupils feel very positive and proud when seeing their work displayed and this reaction in pupils is one of the strategies that teachers can and should use to boost their pupils' self-esteem and confidence, and pride in their work.

Repair and renovation

Some physical features of the room may need repair or replacement. The effective teacher will recognise that these improvements, while out of his/her immediate ability to secure, are vital to the creation of a positive climate for learning. The effective teacher will then ensure that verbal and written requests to renovate the room are made to the line-manager and SLT in order to create and enhance the learning environment. The key action point is that the teacher will aim to secure the desired improvement, and not assume that his/her need will be known and prioritised by those people in the school who have influence in how budgets are spent.

Point for reflection

Use the following checklist as a prompt for judging the strengths and weaknesses of the physical learning environment in which the teacher and pupils operate.

The physical learning environment			
Features	Yes	Needs Attention	No
• Do the pupils' sitting arrangements allow for quick rearranging into different groupings?			
• Are all pupils able to see the board?			
• Is there a seating plan displayed and followed for all classes that use the room?			
• Is the furniture stable and in a good state of repair?			
• Is the surface of the floor level and its covering safe?			
• Are there blinds at the windows?			

(Continued)

• Are the blinds in a good state of repair?			
• Is the decoration of the room in good condition?			
• Are there sufficient numbers of display boards?			
• Do you have sufficient resources to regularly change your displays?			
• Are keywords displayed and clear to all pupils wherever they sit?			
• Is guidance for pupils on how to improve their work displayed, and is it clear wherever a pupil is sitting?			
• Is pupils' work displayed?			
• Are there clear areas for specific uses in the room, and are these identified for pupils?			
• Are there adequate storage facilities for pupils' coats and bags?			
• Are the teacher's resources for use by the pupils readily available and in good working order?			

We all respond, both consciously and subconsciously, to the physical environment we find ourselves in. In considering the factors that are influential in determining the pupils' behaviour and attitudes towards learning, it is clear that the space in which learning happens needs to be safe, well maintained and welcoming. The effective teacher will ensure that the conditions reflect the features we have described.

5

Using performance reviews to develop teacher performance

The full potential of performance management reviews to support the development of some teachers and to reverse the under-performance of others, has not been realised despite its mandatory status in schools. The statutory performance management process for teachers in mainstream schools in England and Wales has been designed to:

- focus attention on more effective teaching and leadership to benefit pupils, teachers and schools;
- help raise standards;
- increase teachers' job satisfaction and develop professionalism and expertise;
- set a framework for teachers, and their team leaders, to agree and review priorities and objectives within the overall framework of a school's improvement plans;
- support teachers by ensuring regular professional discussions with their team leaders about their work and professional development.

The concept of performance management

The concept of performance management remains one of the most important and formative developments in the leadership and management of staff.

Performance management is a strategic and integrated process that delivers sustained success to organisations by improving the performance of the people who work in them and by developing the capabilities of individual contributors and teams.

(Armstrong, 2000)   **75**

Table 5.1 *Preconditions for effective performance management*

Clarify the role	Discuss and agree the teacher's key result areas and capability requirements. This means setting out the:
	• purpose of the teacher's role, i.e. clarifying what the postholder is expected to do.
	• key result areas – defining the main output areas of the role; and
	• key capabilities – indicating what the teacher has to be able to do and the behaviour required to perform the role effectively.
Define expectations	Define what the teacher has to achieve in the form of job objectives, how performance will be measured and the capabilities needed to deliver the expected results.
Develop the teacher's individual plan	Set out the actions individuals need to take in order to develop their knowledge, skills and understanding.
Implement the action	Implement the action agreed in the teacher's individual plan and provide ongoing feedback through progress reviews.
Review the impact	Formally evaluate the teacher's performance, covering achievements, progress and barriers as the basis for a revised set of objectives.

In most schools, performance management has now developed from being a one-off, annual appraisal into a dynamic, ongoing process focusing on teachers' improvement objectives, underpinned with systematic support. Performance management establishes the vital link between the school's strategic goals for further improvement and the staff, whose role is to help implement them. Performance management achieves this by helping to:

- convert strategic goals into objectives and targets for teams and individuals;
- manage the process systematically through regular performance reviews; and
- support the performance and development of staff.

Vital preconditions of effective performance management reviews are set out in Table 5.1.

A continuous self-reviewing cycle

Performance management is a continuous self-renewing cycle based upon a review meeting that requires clear and open communication between the school (represented by team leaders) and the teacher, in order to plan for the future. The process involves the stages and main activities set out in Figure 5.1.

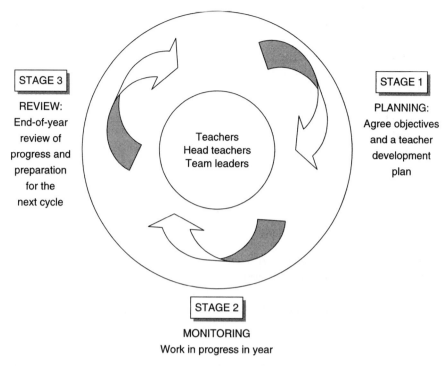

Figure 5.1 *The performance management cycle (adapted from DfEE, 2000)*

Stage 1: Planning

Planning is a pivotal first step in establishing a continuous self-reviewing cycle since it provides opportunities for teachers and line-managers to identify:

- the purpose of the individual's role, the key result areas and the key capabilities;
- the actions that need to be taken to secure high quality performance;
- when these actions are best taken;
- a staged process for achieving the objectives through agreed actions;
- how the actions and tasks might be carried out;
- the resources required to support the agreed actions;
- how progress towards achieving the goals is to be monitored; and
- the deadline for achieving the desired change/objective.

The benefits of the planning process can be enhanced greatly if the teacher and the line-manager are both aware of appropriate details relating to the:

- school's aims and mission statement;
- school's improvement plan;

77

- team/phase/subject area plans;
- self-review documents (school, department, subject, individual e.g. self-evaluation form);
- statistical data – internal, external (e.g. PANDA, LEA profile, teacher assessments, national test results);
- individual pupils' targets;
- feedback from lesson observations;
- school self-evaluation;
- job descriptions;
- continuing professional development (CPD) records; and
- Threshold Assessment feedback.

Point for reflection

Identify those areas where you have a secure knowledge of the teacher's work and contribution to the school.

List those areas where your knowledge is less secure and consider how you would set about getting the information needed.

Throughout the planning stage, the team leader and the teacher need to be aware of issues of equality – the team leader's views, conduct, expectations need to be seen as being fair to all and consistent with the views and conduct of other team leaders.

Agreeing objectives

Following discussion about and agreement of the objectives, it is crucial for the teacher and the line-manager to:

- record the objectives, together with the strategies for meeting them, in an individual plan which can be referred to and updated throughout the cycle;
- identify and record the form of the professional development activities that will best support the achievement of the agreed objectives; and
- identify the support and resources needed to achieve the objectives.

Teachers' objectives need to be SMART (Specific; Measurable; Achievable; Realistic; Time-lined) and clearly linked to the school's priorities as set out in the school improvement plan, as well as to the teacher's personal professional needs.

Agreeing a teacher's individual plan

As part of the planning meeting, the teacher and the team leader will need to agree an individual written plan like the one shown in Table 5.2. This will identify the skills and/or knowledge to help the teacher perform more effectively and set specific actions for developing these. Individual plans should be the result of candid discussions and, wherever possible, should be mutually agreed – the plan is more likely to be implemented if not imposed by the team leader.

Team leaders will find it helpful to:

- facilitate, guide and support rather than impose or coerce;
- devise a plan that is concise and addresses the key issues, identifying the key actions which will help the teacher to achieve improvement objectives;
- monitor the plan and gather evidence of progress towards the achievement of objectives;
- be realistic about what is achievable;
- take account of the resources, including the time, available;
- gauge the level of professional support required to achieve the objectives;
- identify the teacher's professional development needs, the nature of the activity required and how this can be provided;
- reach agreement with the teacher about the expected outcomes of the professional development experience and how they are to be measured;
- know the full range of CPD opportunities, including the school's own expertise; and
- ensure that access to the development activity is open to those teachers who need it (within budgetary constraints).

Stage 2: Monitoring

Effective performance management requires the regular and systematic monitoring of progress and commitment to ongoing support.

(Jones, 2001)

The team leader is responsible for monitoring the teacher's progress against the agreed objectives, even though a substantial responsibility for self-review falls to the teacher. Monitoring activity might include:

- lesson observations;
- informal discussions;
- formal meetings and discussions;
- checks against individual plans;
- scrutiny of pupils' work; and
- analysis of test/examination results.

Stage 3: Review

To ensure maximum benefit from the performance review, it is well worth paying particular attention to the following points:

Table 5.2 *Drawing up an individual plan*

Name: ☐   Jan Lomas   Date: ☐ 1/3/06

Objective: ☐   To improve your management of the pupils' behaviour in your class

How will I get there?	Activities	When? Start? Finish?	How will I know that I have succeeded?
Getting the children's attention	• Projecting voice at right pitch • No talking over children's talk • Have something useful/interesting to say	Immediate start – ongoing	Children quickly pay attention – listen carefully
Providing a work programme which engages the attention of all pupils	• Ensure that work is pitched at the right levels for all pupils • Ensure that the pro-gramme is sufficiently active, and of interest to all pupils • Positive, constructive feedback	ASAP – ongoing	Lessons engage and motivate all pupils
Clarifying strate-gies for rewards and sanctions	• Agree classroom rules with pupils – discuss acceptable/unacceptable behaviour	Beginning of next half-term – complete within 2 weeks, but subject to amendment	Agreed classroom rules displayed prominently in classroom – children keen to adhere to them
Reinforcing positive behaviour	• Where possible, ignore unacceptable behaviour, taking action where absolutely necessary	ASAP – ongoing	Tone, atmosphere in classroom of good standard
Reducing unnecessary noise in the classroom	• Caretaker asked to check chair-leg rubbers • Use group strategies for moving around classroom	End of term – during holidays ASAP – ongoing	Reduced noise levels in classroom

Resources/Support required: Outcomes expected:

• Help needed to plan work of SEN group – John, Sarah, Tony
• Discuss behaviour management with school educational psychologist
• Attend course on 'Planning for the Curriculum'

Agreed monitoring activities:

- The timing of the review should be agreed well in advance to allow the team leader and the teacher to organise their various schedules and to prepare for the review.
- The review meeting should be arranged for a time when both teachers and team leaders can devote their full attention to the review process.

- To avoid cramming and rushing, the review itself should be given a long enough time slot. It is unwise to go beyond a two-hour session.
- The review should be carried out in a quiet room, free of interruptions by people and telephones. Arrange the chairs so that you are sitting not quite opposite each other, with a low table between you both to put papers on. Some light refreshments also help.
- The review should start with a short, informal chat on general matters just to ensure both parties are relaxed.
- The review proper should then begin with points arising from the teacher's self-review, and earlier lesson observation. This discussion should be broadened to include other topics and issues, including the teacher's strengths and weaknesses, opportunities and problems, under-achievements, ideas for changes and possible future objectives.
- The points made and agreed should be summarised in the review statement and the session closed.

Point for reflection

Look at the way in which you conduct performance reviews. What are your strengths and weaknesses as a reviewer?

Providing a range of opportunities for CPD

Establishing a clear focus for professional development is an essential element of the performance review. For example, the review meeting should help all teachers, irrespective of their experience and status, to consider how they can improve their professional practice and how they will be supported in this. Research, such as that reported in *Learning and Teaching: A Strategy for Professional Development* (DfES, 2001) shows that professional development is most likely to lead to successful changes in teachers' practice where development involves the following elements:

- A focus upon specific teaching and learning issues.
- Opportunities for teachers to reflect on what they know and do already.
- Opportunities for teachers to: understand the rationale behind new ideas and approaches; see theory demonstrated in practice; and be exposed to new expertise.
- Sustained opportunities to experiment with new ideas and approaches, so that teachers can work out the implications for their own subject, pupils, school and community.
- Opportunities for teachers to have some control over how new strategies and ideas might work, building on their existing knowledge and skills.

- Regular and systematic coaching and feedback on their professional practice over a period of time.
- Situations where teachers are supported by their head teacher or subject leaders and through participation in wider networks.

Yet, for many teachers, the image of CPD is still of one-off events or short courses, often away from the school, of variable quality and relevance, delivered by a range of external providers. As teachers and their team leaders begin to set development objectives as part of the performance management process, and consider how best to meet them, there is real value in thinking **first** about creating opportunities within their own school and, through links with other schools, to learn from, and with, other effective colleagues. Imaginative use of a range of professional development activities can develop a teacher's performance. Teachers could benefit from:

- observing a colleague teach;
- joining or establishing a working group to consider an aspect of teaching and learning, e.g. group work, independent learning;
- mentoring from an experienced colleague;
- high quality training from someone with relevant expertise, e.g. pupil behaviour consultant, followed by support in the classroom;
- consulting appropriate websites, e.g. the Department for Education and Skills (DfES), the National College for School Leadership (NCSL), the Teacher Development Agency (TDA), the General Teaching Council (GTC);
- collaborating on extra-curricular activities with an experienced and skilled colleague;
- working with visiting professionals, e.g. speech therapist, educational psychologist;
- working with an examinations board;
- teaching a wide range of ability groups;
- carrying out a piece of action research into an aspect of teaching and learning; and
- making use of the expertise of an Advanced Skills Teacher (AST).

Point for reflection

Draw on your experience to think of examples of effective **in-school** opportunities to develop and/or change professional practice.

- How can teachers be made aware of these opportunities?
- How might they be encouraged to take responsibility for improving their professional practice?
- How might they be helped to judge the impact of CPD on their professional practice?

Coaching skills for team leaders

This section sets out to help the reader understand the purposes and benefits of coaching and the skills necessary to coach effectively. Coaching has for some time been actively used in a business environment in the context of raising performance. Research in education management has also defined the benefits of coaching for education (Jones, 2005). Performance management brings into focus the importance of developing and enhancing coaching skills. According to Megginson and Boydell (1979) coaching is:

> *a process in which a manager, through direct discussion and guided activity, helps a colleague to solve a problem, or to do a task better than would otherwise have been the case.*

In essence, coaching is about helping people to improve beyond their present capability and is an important element in the performance management process because it offers opportunities for:

- further learning and development in the workplace;
- questioning and listening;
- gaining feedback on performance issues;
- discussion about performance issues and the knowledge and skills required to resolve them;
- working on a particular issue or problem or opportunity, as a mutual problem-solving situation;
- testing the data already held by the learner;
- contributing additional data or alternative views about existing data in relation to particular situations, priorities for action, options for decisions, etc.;
- demonstrating, modelling and explaining more than telling; and
- modelling effective styles and skills by the team leader in the role of coach.

The role of the team leader in coaching is key to the development of a high-performing team. Coaching skills have direct relevance to activities undertaken in monitoring and to reviewing overall performance.

Point for reflection

It is highly likely that we have all experienced coaching at some stage in our development, for example in learning to ride a bike; in learning to sing, play a musical instrument; in learning sporting skills such as swimming; in learning different skills when taking up a new job.

(Continued)   **83**

(Continued)

Reflect on a situation when you were coached or provided coaching for someone else. From your experience, consider the:

- characteristics of the coaching process;
- purposes of coaching;
- benefits of coaching.

Knowledge, skills and behaviours required for coaching

Table 5.3 and the reflection point below have been designed to enable participants to identify the knowledge, skills and behaviours underpinning successful coaching.

Point for reflection

Reflect on a personal experience of successful coaching either as a learner or as a coach.

- What was the coaching situation and its purpose?
- What style of coaching was used, e.g. was it directive or non-directive?
- What features of coaching were most significant in providing learning opportunities?
- Why was the experience successful and how did you know?
- What knowledge and skills contributed to this success?
- What behaviours contributed to the success?

Styles and skills of coaching

There are different styles of coaching – for example **directive** coaching, which emphasises:

- explicit guidance;
- instruction on 'how to'; and
- the provision of data.

Another style is non-directive or **elicitive** coaching, which is more likely to lead to ownership and learning in the long term.

Coaching is one of the most powerful interpersonal relationships. To be an effective coach, the team leader needs to build trusting relationships and should

Table 5.3   *Knowledge, skills and behaviours underpinning successful coaching*

Knowledge and understanding	• Context of the school • School improvement plan – priorities identified • Range of data providing evidence and information • Ethos and culture of the school • Own knowledge and experience as classroom practitioner • Own knowledge and experience as manager/team leader • Knowledge of the job context of the individual being coached • Knowledge of the opportunities/constraints for this individual • Knowledge/Understanding of range of opportunities for professional development • Knowledge/Understanding of access to professional development • Knowledge/Understanding of resource implications
Skills	• Communication: listening skills, e.g. active listening, reflective listening, open listening • Appropriate questioning strategies • Drawing out, recognising and revealing feelings • Giving feedback • Negotiating and agreeing objectives • Reviewing • Ability to challenge and confront • Analytical skills • Organisational and administrative skills • Evaluative skills – ability to reflect and learn from experiences and encourage others to do this
Behaviours	• Integrity • Honesty • Sincerity • Genuine interest and concern • Trust • Openness • Understanding • Empathy • Willing to share own skills • Willing to acknowledge own difficulties • Willing to challenge/set expectations • Willing to confront • Willing to reflect and learn from experiences

understand that good listening is, without question, the most important skill in coaching. Focused listening is crucial for establishing such a relationship because it involves investing in understanding before being understood. Individuals may know exactly what **they** want to say. They may express themselves clearly, but if the team leader understands differently, the teacher will feel misunderstood and communication will break down. Table 5.4 summarises the elements of the

Table 5.4 *Summary of the coaching process*

Coaching Process	Skills	Knowledge	Tips
Identify the gap/Respond to requests	Listening Questioning Reflecting Gathering information Observing	Knowledge of the job and potential areas of difficulty. Knowledge of the individual's job role.	Make sure you validate all information against agreed levels of performance.
Consider learning styles and barriers	Listening Questioning Reflecting Gathering information	Knowledge of potential learning options. Awareness of your learning style and how that may impact on a coaching activity.	Use the learning styles questionnaire – it's fun and can provide valuable information.
Agree and note objectives	Listening Questioning Objective setting and writing Task and job analysis	Principles of SMART objectives.	Use action verbs list to help produce SMART objectives. Remember objectives need to reflect agreed performance levels.
Discuss and agree learning options	Listening Questioning Reflecting Gathering information Matching learning options to learning styles	Awareness of a variety of learning options and how these relate to the potential coaching session.	Try to encourage the learner to identify how the coaching session should run.
Consider the planning of the session and agree the plan	Listening Questioning Time management Resource management Negotiation skills Written communication	Knowledge of resources available, people, materials and of job roles and responsibilities and working patterns. Planning and preparing demonstrations, presentations and discussions.	Ensure you make enough time for the session and remember to inform anyone else who may be affected.
Action the plan	Listening Reflecting Questioning Encouraging Recording skills Feedback skills	How to analyse tasks. How people learn. What motivates individuals. Subject knowledge.	Remember to keep the session learner-centred.
Review the plan	Listening Reflecting Questioning Encouraging Recording skills Feedback skills	Knowledge of the feedback process and how to encourage learner self-assessment.	Review should be ongoing. Provide options and choices and enable the learner to reflect on achievements as well as planning for the future.

Table 5.5   *Coachee learning styles (adapted from Honey and Mumford, 1988)*

Activists	Activists will like the immediacy of problem solving and 'being given help when I need it'. They are much less likely to welcome being asked to collect data, reach their own conclusions and then to plan further action. They prefer 'directive' coaching: 'Give me an answer.' They are unlikely to plan before coaching or review on paper afterwards.
Reflectors	Reflectors are likely to respond well to planned coaching sessions to deal with problems identified in advance, but are less keen on being rushed into a coaching experience to deal with an immediate problem. They are most likely to want to 'take that idea away and think about it' and will be interested in well-presented, balanced feedback – less likely to move into the concluding and planning next steps stage. They are more likely to prefer non-directive coaching which enables them to proceed at their own pace.
Theorists	Theorists are likely to respond happily where the coach is operating from the same values, models, beliefs and concepts as they are. If this is not so, they are likely to debate and argue rather than adapt and use. They will judge the coach on the relevance and quality of the experiences and could use a learning log, if given theory and structure behind the discipline.
Pragmatists	Pragmatists are likely to see coaching as being particularly useful because it is centred on immediate, relevant work issues. They may possibly leap too quickly to adopt an apparently valid technique or skill, without fully testing it through the reflecting and concluding stage of the learning cycle. They could accept either directive or non-directive coaching depending on the situation: 'That really showed me the answer to today's big problem' or 'It was useful to be made to work out for myself what the cause of the problem was'.

coaching process and the skills and knowledge needed to coach effectively. Some useful tips are also provided to help the reader avoid some common pitfalls.

Learning styles and the coaching relationship

There is a strong impact on learning preferences in the coaching relationship. Because coaching is a learning opportunity, individual learning preferences need to be considered as part of this. Strong learning style preferences are likely to bring about different kinds of coaching and different reactions to coaching (outlined in Table 5.5). Honey and Mumford (1988) have identified four styles of learning. Knowledge of each of the styles might enable the coach to:

- identify implications for the coaching relationship;
- help the individuals to identify the best options to meet their learning needs; and
- use the learning style preferences to enable people to understand and to put their differences to better use rather than being frustrated and upset by them.

Table 5.6 *Coach learning styles*

Activists	Activists are unlikely to plan ahead or provide structured discussion and will move quickly into the 'what to do'.
Reflectors	Reflectors are more likely to ask questions and cause the learner to think than to provide immediate solutions.
Theorists	Theorists are likely to present strong individual views and to seek to generalise from personal experience or from adopted models or theories.
Pragmatists	Pragmatists will tend to focus on issues of direct relevance and to offer guidance on appropriate techniques.

It is important to clarify the purpose of the coaching relationship at the out-set, otherwise it may be interpreted as remedial rather than developmental. Coaching needs to be identified as a learning opportunity. As a coach, the team leader is acting as:

- a role model – modelling how to tackle problems and how to behave as a coach; and
- a provider of learning – by giving the opportunity for clear and explicit discussion of problems and issues.

Coaches will provide help according to their own learning styles. It will be important to be aware of different learning styles in managing coaching relationships. We will also need to remember the part our own learning style will play and the potential for our learning style to become our coaching style. (Table 5.6. sets out the implications of our preferred learning styles for the way in which we approach coaching.) Taking learning styles into account will help us to manage coaching relationships even more successfully.

Building trust

The quality of a relationship between two people is critical to the success of performance management. With little or no trust, even the most technically correct system will not enable feedback and coaching to be effective. The major 'trust builders' are set out in Table 5.7.

Effective listening skills and barriers to good listening

The following body language helps to demonstrate active listening:

- appropriate eye contact;
- non-verbal prompts, which encourage the person to continue speaking, e.g. nodding occasionally; using appropriate facial expressions, in response to

Table 5.7   *Trust builders*

Clarity of communication	Giving clear messages – both oral and written.
Establishing clear and positive expectations	Being clear about what is expected, forming expectations so that people feel positive and supported.
Listening	Attending **actively** to what others say.
Openness	Being willing to explore new possibilities and new experiences.
Admitting mistakes	Showing a willingness to admit to mistakes you've made and making amends rather than maintaining an image of perfection and arrogance and denying responsibility for mistakes or placing blame on others.
Disclosing	Being willing to share useful information even when it might make you vulnerable (e.g. a mistake that taught a useful lesson).
Valuing	Respecting the view points, ideas and ideals of others; actually **hearing** what others say.
Involving others	Drawing out the opinions, feelings, ideas, skills of others and asking for their help and participation.
Making and keeping commitments; honouring expectations	Taking promises seriously and delivering on those made offering to help move work forward; confirming who, what and when.
Sensitivity	Being authentic and honest, 'walking like one talks', saying identical things to one's face and behind one's back; being straightforward instead of 'playing games'.
Technical competence	Being respected as capable of doing the job well – skilful in some aspects.

the person's feelings rather than your own reactions to them; tolerating silence to communicate patience;
- sitting at an angle or adjacent to, rather than opposite, the person;
- adopting an appropriate stance, e.g. open rather than folded arms; and
- avoiding distractions, such as tapping pencils etc.

Good listeners are able to:

- Focus the discussion: 'Which is the most important thing that we've talked about in the last ten minutes?'
- Use verbal prompts such as: 'Ye-es, go on. I see. Can you tell me more about that . . . ?'
- Use the 'playback' technique, i.e. repeat a keyword – one word to avoid breaking the train of thought.
- Ask questions to clarify meaning such as: 'How do you feel about it? Can you give me an example? What does that mean to you?'
- Paraphrase what has been said to further discussion without interrupting thinking: 'So you felt very pleased with that, you . . . ?'
- Summarise what has been said to the satisfaction of the speaker.

Barriers to good listening include:

- *'Open ears–closed mind' listening.* Jumping to conclusions about what the speaker will say, therefore closing the mind because 'we will learn nothing new'.
- *On–off listening.* This is where we are using the time to think about what we are going to say next; when this happens we are not listening to what is being said.
- *'Glazed look' listening.* We are looking at the speaker, but not listening because our minds are on other things.
- *'Red-flag' listening.* We block out or interrupt the speaker because key-words have engendered an emotional response.
- *'Obviously' listening.* Repeating facts, consequently missing new facts.
- *Avoiding the issue.* Not listening to or asking for clarification because the subject appears too difficult or complex.
- *'Matter over mind' listening.* We have already decided on the outcome, therefore refuse to have our own ideas and points of view challenged.
- *Focusing on the subject instead of the speaker.* Details and facts about an incident become more important than what people are saying about themselves. There is a danger here of missing key facts and speakers' expressions.
- *Allowing external distractions (corridor noise, telephone, etc.) to take over our attention.*

Point for reflection

Think of a coaching session that you have recently participated in. Use the following criteria to help you judge its success.

- During the session, what **evidence** is there of effective coaching?
- How well was the purpose of the interview clarified?
- How well was the coachee put at his/her ease?
- What types of questions were asked (open, closed, probing, leading, multiple)?
- How well were views of the coachee listened to?
- What evidence was there of effective listening skills?
- How well did the coach and the coachee work together on options and solutions for performance development?
- How well did the coach summarise and reach agreement on future actions?
- What other observations were you able to make?

Using questioning techniques effectively

Well-developed questioning techniques enable teachers to:

- be fully involved in performance review;
- identify their own strengths, weaknesses and professional development needs; and
- play an active part in deciding the way forward.

Using the right questions is key to providing effective feedback. We make regular use of a variety of questioning techniques on a day-to-day basis. The most common types of questions used are set out in Table 5.8.

Point for reflection

Using one of the vignettes presented earlier in this chapter, focus on two of the teacher's strengths or two of the areas for improvement and frame questions/statements based on (a) the elicitive form of feedback; and (b) the directive form of feedback.

Giving feedback

The importance of feedback in effecting better performance can never be overestimated. Therefore, it is crucial that team leaders understand the skills necessary for giving feedback that will improve performance while sustaining the teacher's sense of self-worth. Reviews of performance and subsequent improvement of performance will be most effective when the teacher is an active participant in the process. Teachers need to have their successes recognised, leading to a sense of self-worth and self-fulfilment. This section of the chapter will make you aware of the different styles of feedback.

Strategies for giving constructive feedback

Being absolutely clear about the **need** to address under-performance is an essential basis for doing this well. Having a strategy or 'code of practice' for giving constructive criticism will help to overcome personal sensitivity. The following points are set out to help you identify strategies for giving constructive criticism:

- Hold a meeting to discuss the matter as soon as possible.
- Hold the meeting in private – criticism should **never** be made publicly.
- Ensure that the purpose of the meeting is clear and come straight to the point: 'We are here to discuss ...'
- Ensure that the teacher has the opportunity to contribute his/her views of what happened.

Table 5.8   *Types of questions*

Open questions – are designed to elicit as much information as possible.	• Which part of your teaching do you enjoy most? • How would you describe your experience of . . . ? • What would you want to gain from this course? • What do you think would be the best way to take this forward? • What are the advantages of using this one? • How did you overcome those?
Probing questions – are designed to go deeper into the issue, in order to gain quality information.	• In what way? • How did you feel when you had completed that work? • What makes that part of the job interesting/more satisfying/difficult? • Will you expand on that a little? • Why is that important? • What makes it helpful/difficult to work in that way?
Reflective questions – are questions which check out understanding and reflect information back to the job holder in order to help him/her develop the issue further:	• So are you saying that . . . ? • Are you telling me that . . . ? • If I were to summarise what you've said, would I be right in saying. . . ?
Closed questions – can be used to gather information, or to check facts.	• Have you used this computer program often? • What resources do you use for . . . ? • Where did you find this information? Closed questions lead to specific information or the reply 'yes' or 'no'. They may need to be followed up with more open questions: • Have you used this reading text before? • Are there any disadvantages?
Multiple questions – when two or more questions are asked at the same time. They are best avoided, as they are often confusing. Usually only one question will be answered.	• Will you tell me what you've done best and what you'd like to improve on? • Are you happy with the agenda, would you like to add something or do you think we should approach it differently?
Leading questions – can be frustrating if used too often or inappropriately, but they can sometimes be useful for exerting influence. You are likely to get a positive response whether the teacher agrees with you or not. It is important to follow up with an open question.	• I'm sure you can see the advantages of this, can't you? • What do think these advantages may be? (follow-up) • Don't you think that would be a good idea? • So, how do we put it into practice? (follow-up)

- Agree on the facts, based on **evidence**.
- Focus on the **practice**, never on the person.
- Ensure that the teacher understands why improvement is important.
- Discuss and agree how improvement will be effected – what support will be given.
- Agree a date to review performance.
- 'Build bridges' – remind the teacher about aspects of his/her work which are valued and which make a contribution.

Point for reflection

The purpose of this activity is to help you to identify key principles to support the management of discussions about under-performance.
 Reflect on a situation where you gave or received 'constructive criticism'. How did you feel? What was the outcome?
 Identify key principles to underpin discussions about under–performance.

Line-managers and teachers usually find confrontation difficult and, understandably, try to avoid it. There are several reasons for this, not least that:

- many find it difficult to criticise peer professionals;
- they do not wish to compromise working relationships; and
- they have had personal experience of negative feedback which was damaging or did not lead to improvement.

Teachers are aware of the damage that can be caused by insensitive feedback. They are also aware of the problems that will be caused if unacceptable behaviours and practices are not confronted. It is essential that skills in providing constructive criticism are acquired and practised – less stress for the person giving the feedback, less anxiety and increased motivation for the recipient.

Point for reflection

Reflect upon a situation where you may have given or received constructive criticism. How did you feel? What was the outcome? What are the principles for holding people accountable and giving constructive criticism?

Styles of feedback

Effective feedback:

- involves staff in appraising their own performance and identifying professional development needs;
- allows the teacher and the reviewer to introduce views and information about topics which they both feel are important;
- encourages the teacher to identify what s/he is good at and areas where further support is needed;
- gives the reviewer opportunities to reinforce good performance; and
- prepares the ground for constructive discussion around improvement of areas where performance is not as good.

Point for reflection

Reflect on your own experiences of a recent feedback to you **or** your experience of giving feedback to another person.

- What was good about the experience?
- What was disagreeable about the experience?
- What made it disagreeable?
- How could it have been improved?

As strange as it may seem, many people, especially teachers, are reluctant to say what they have done well. There may be a need to lead the responses, encouraging the teacher by judicious questioning. In giving feedback, **do not** concentrate only on what needs to be improved – this will damage the teacher's confidence. Some may be reluctant to identify areas where their performance is not as good as they would want. The reviewer should not avoid these areas but use accurate information about the teacher's performance, describing relevant incidents, to provide basis for discussion. The discussion should be honest but sensitive and unambiguous. It should not leave the teacher feeling uncomfortable because of being unable to divine what is in the reviewer's mind.

The **elicitive** form of feedback, using questioning skills, encourages the teacher to think about the work that has been done and how to maintain or improve performance. Elicitive feedback encourages the teacher to play a full part in the review and to take ownership of his/her own performance and development needs. It is most likely to lead to positive improvement.

The technique of 'telling' or describing facts, known as **directive** feedback, can feel more comfortable and can be used to reinforce points already made by the teacher. In directive feedback the reviewer tells the teacher:

Table 5.9 *The STAR model for gauging coaching success*

SITUATION	What is the current context and position? What does the teacher want to improve? (e.g. to improve management of behaviour) What will help the teacher to achieve this? What strategies could the teacher use? What training and professional development does the teacher need?
TASK	The teacher will, with the help of the team leader: • observe X and Y teaching these pupils • identify effective classroom management strategies • discuss these and explore further with X and Y • investigate other sources of support.
ACTION	What action will the teacher now take? (e.g. plan lessons to make use of identified strategies; try these out in teaching; invite team leader to observe; reflect and evaluate with team leader on outcomes; modify 'tasks' where necessary)
RESULT	• What result is looked for? (e.g. the teacher will have improved his/her classroom management)

- what happened;
- what effect it had on performance;
- what s/he liked or didn't like and why;
- what s/he would like the teacher to do differently or more of.

The best feedback uses a balance of 'elicitive' and 'directive' approaches. After feedback, the reviewer and the teacher need to consider what is to happen next and to decide objectives for future performance development.

Gauging the success of the coaching relationship

A useful way of measuring success in the coaching relationship is the use of **STAR**. The acronym **STAR** refers to Situation, Task, Action, Result (see Table 5.9).

The STAR model provides a structure for utilising the skills, knowledge and behaviour required for effective coaching. If successful, both individual and coach achieve professional growth and development.

Point for reflection

Choose one of the following two scenarios. From what you have read in this chapter, what skills and approaches would you use to develop a meaningful coaching relationship?

(Continued)

(Continued)

Scenario 1 (primary)

You are the Key Stage 2 Co-ordinator at Wilsby Primary School where you have been teaching for nine years. You are Pat Smart's Team Leader and are impressed by how quickly she was able to contribute to the school as a Year 3 teacher following her induction year at another school. Pat has been teaching a Year 6 class since September and is managing well with the different demands of the curriculum and assessment. However, she is finding the behaviour of some pupils in the class very challenging – this was evident in a recent lesson that you observed.

Pat Smart

Pat is in her third year of teaching and has been on the staff of Wilsby for the last two years. To date, her experience of teaching has been in Year 3, but this year she has been given a Year 6 class. Pat is quite pleased with the way she has coped with the curriculum and assessment of her class, but she is now finding the challenging behaviour of some of the pupils in the class difficult to handle. The Head Teacher has received a complaint from parents concerned about the progress of their child, 'because Ms Smart seems to tolerate poor behaviour'.

   Both you and Pat have been made aware of this complaint. You have been asked by the Head Teacher to discuss the matter with Pat and agree appropriate action that will help improve her performance in this area.

Scenario 2 (secondary)

You are Head of the Communications Faculty and Chris Saville's team leader. Chris has been Head of the English Department for three years and with the introduction of Performance Management has been appointed team leader of the four other teachers in the department. You are aware that Chris is not looking forward to holding performance reviews with his team – you think his reluctance comes from lack of confidence and not rejection of the process. Redstock High is an Investors in People (IIP) school and the culture is one of creative and continuing professional development. You have invited Chris to meet with you to discuss ways forward.

(Continued)

(Continued)

Christine Saville

Chris has been Head of the English Department at Redstock High School for two years. As part of his performance management responsibilities, he will review the performance of the four teachers in his department. He agrees with the rationale and process of performance management – Redstock is an IIP school and the culture is one of professional development – but lacks the confidence to tell his colleagues that he is worried about the quality of learning taking place in their classrooms. His colleagues, who are quite a bit older than him, teach in what he regards as a highly traditional way. This manner of teaching is beginning to impact on the behaviour of some students who often complain about being bored in class.

You have suggested a coaching session to help support Chris with his task.

Promoting teacher development – a whole-school approach to CPD

A number of useful publications already exist on the topic of continuing professional development (CPD) and the opportunities now available to teachers to enhance their skills, knowledge and understanding. The intention of this chapter is not to add to that resource but to focus on one whole-school approach to the provision of CPD that we have found to be particularly effective in meeting the needs of staff in schools.

Meeting the development needs of teachers

When newly qualified teachers (NQTs) are appointed, they are required to follow an induction process in order to complete their NQT year and gain Qualified Teacher Status (QTS). A combination of regular professional discussion with a mentor and staff development activities are central features of these induction programmes. The provision of a systematic programme of induction for other staff appointed to the school is equally important, but too often this amounts to little more than a cursory session with the line-manager and the allocation of a staff handbook. This can happen because line-managers are often too busy, indifferent to the task, lack the confidence and skills to fulfill this role, and might even believe that induction programmes are inappropriate for more experienced staff.

Newly appointed middle leaders, in particular, are often expected to just 'get on with it' and can find themselves suddenly under pressure when they realise that the status and control they may have once enjoyed in a previous post does not automatically accompany them to their new post. However, staff members are the most important resource for improvement that schools have at their disposal and investing time in the induction of new and existing staff can help to:

- clarify the school's professional expectations of teachers;
- get across the message that they work in an organisation which values individuals and supports their development;
- create a culture in which open professional dialogue focusing on improvement is the norm;
- enable teachers to constantly improve and develop their skills;
- create the expectation that teaching is a profession that is constantly adapting to new situations; and
- provide a supportive context in which teachers can develop and experiment with new skills and new approaches.

Schools can face problems when, as is often the case, the new teacher is the only new member of staff starting at a particular time, or there are several new staff but they are at different career stages and have different induction needs, and lastly, there is no set induction programme for new staff to follow.

One approach to developing teacher performance is for schools to build a culture of professional development through the creation of a Professional Development Group (PDG). In small primary schools, this can be achieved by collaborating with one or more similar schools to create such a group, e.g. clusters, partnership, collaboratives, federations.

The professional development group

Purpose

The purpose of having a Professional Development Group is to create a forum in which all aspects of teachers' professional development can be considered regularly and systematically. The group acts as a focus for the planning, monitoring and review of the professional development of all staff whether newly qualified, new to the school, under-performing, stuck, or progressing. As such, it could make a considerable contribution to the continuing improvement of the organisation and to the development of teachers' performance.

Function

The main functions of the Professional Development Group are to:

- identify its own training and development needs;
- identify the training needs of all involved in teaching within the organisation;
- plan, organise and deliver training to meet the needs of all staff;

- plan and organise whole-school training to meet whole-school needs;
- induct new staff;
- support NQTs and young teachers in their early years in the profession;
- develop whole-staff training for new initiatives;
- support under-performing teachers through coaching and mentoring;
- update the skills of individual teachers;
- pre-empt the situation where an experienced teacher 'gets into a rut' or stuck;
- provide teachers who have progressed across the threshold with a forum for sharing their enhanced skills with others by coaching or mentoring other staff; and
- provide a cross-phase, cross-curricular or cross-school forum for professional discussion and planning.

Ideally, the Professional Development Group would have an important impact on the culture of the school, creating an expectation that teachers have the right to receive support and that they should continue to develop professionally throughout their teaching career.

Composition

The composition of the Professional Development Group will, inevitably, be varied and will differ from school to school and from time to time. However, senior leaders may strongly advise that the group is made up of a core membership in order to be truly representative of the staff for a specified period of time, e.g. staff new to the school, NQTs, Fast Track teachers, teachers who have progressed through the threshold, ASTs.

Other staff could be asked to join for a period of time as part of a support plan to help them overcome difficulties and the group could be open to any member of staff who wants to join for his/her own professional development. Staff who had been asked to join the group as part of a support plan would not need to declare this – they could simply join the group as apparent 'volunteers'.

Chairing

It is likely that the school's Professional Development Co-ordinator (PDC) would want to be a member of the group but thought should be given to the chairing of the group if the PDC is a senior leader. For example, chairing this group could be a development opportunity for a middle leader, an aspiring deputy head, or for a teacher who is approaching or who has passed through the threshold. The fact that the chair of the group is *not* a senior leader can itself be a powerful self-development message and it can contribute to the group's sense of self-empowerment. Whoever is chosen to chair this group, s/he will need highly developed interpersonal skills to encourage openness and professional dialogue and to consult with the PDC and other senior leaders. A Professional Development Group will not work well if:

- it is seen to blame individuals for professional failings;
- it only seeks external solutions to problems;
- it is not proactive and imaginative; and
- the chair is not able to command professional respect from staff.

Identifying continuing professional development needs

The group will need to do two important things:

- identify the training needs of the less experienced members of the PDG.
- identify training needs throughout the school (including non-teachers in support roles).

This can be done:

- through discussion with staff;
- by referring to the school improvement plan;
- using the anonymous list of training needs emerging from the performance management process;
- by referring to a previous Ofsted report;
- by referring to self-evaluation strategies;
- using a training needs questionnaire; and
- using a mixture of some, or all, of the above.

This needs analysis process is likely to show that the Group and the whole staff have a variety of training and skills needs. Table 6.1 shows some examples of what these training and skills needs are likely to be.

Responding to needs

It is important that members of the PDG discuss the list that emerges from the needs analysis process. The group should be encouraged to try to identify imaginative ways in which these training needs can be met. Where possible, the group will be encouraged to meet group training needs from within the resources of the group, e.g. more experienced staff coaching or mentoring less experienced staff. An example of the annual training plan for a PDG is shown in Table 6.2. This group has chosen to concentrate its annual training plan on two main areas:

Table 6.1   *Training needs of staff*

What training is needed?	Who is likely to need this training?
Understanding and operating school policies and systems	New staff and staff who are struggling to act consistently in line with school policies and systems
Lesson planning and structure	Newly qualified staff, staff who are struggling to plan and structure their lessons effectively
More advanced pedagogic skills (e.g. planning for different teaching and learning styles, thinking skills, accelerated learning, coaching, assessment for learning, the use of new technology)	More experienced staff, staff who are struggling to extend their pedagogic repertoire
Behaviour management – basic techniques	Newly qualified staff, staff who are struggling to establish basic classroom control
Behaviour management – more advanced skills	More experienced staff, staff who are struggling to extend their behaviour management repertoire
Leadership and management skills	Staff who are new to middle management or aspire to middle management
New government/LEA/school initiatives	All staff

- Consistent application and operation of whole-school systems.
- Behaviour management training, both for individual PDG members and across the whole school.

Planning activities

Once the Professional Development Group has identified the activities it wants to engage in for the year, these activities need to be scheduled in the school calendar and included in the School Improvement Plan. The school's Staff Development for School Improvement Plan can then be written. An example has been provided in Table 6.3.

The Professional Development Group will need to:

- plan a programme to meet the training needs of the group, using experienced members of the group and other staff, as necessary, as a resource. This will encourage reflection and learning in a supportive group situation for teachers who are new or struggling, as well as making

Table 6.2 *Example of an annual training plan for a Professional Development Group*

Identified training/ development need	Ways in which development/ training need could be met	What needs to be done to make this happen
Understanding and operating school policies and systems (new staff and staff who are struggling to act consistently in line with school policies and systems).	Training provided by: 1. Head teacher (school aims and values). 2. Manager responsible for pastoral care (pastoral policies and systems). 3. Manager responsible for standards of teaching and learning (teaching and learning policies and systems). 4. Manager responsible for SEN (SEN policy and systems). 5. Manager responsible for administration (administration policy and systems). 6. PDG review and update staff handbook. 7. Joint lesson planning, observation and feedback.	Chair of PDG to speak to relevant managers and set up several sessions where the main policies and systems can be outlined. Individual programmes of support provide by members of the PDG.
Extending the range of behaviour management techniques used by some members of the PDG and by the staff as a whole (particularly newly qualified staff, new staff to the school, and staff who are struggling to establish basic classroom control).	PDG to develop own materials and plan and deliver appropriate behaviour management training both within the PDG and across the whole school.	Chair of PDG to support planning by helping to find or write appropriate training materials.

good use of the expertise of teachers who have progressed through the threshold;

- be encouraged to do at least one activity in the year where PDG members are involved in designing and delivering training for the whole staff. This involvement will give the group a real focus, will make use of the talents of more experienced staff and will encourage all involved to really think through the issues and 'own' the solutions. The PDG can also be given status within the school, e.g. awarding certificates for involvement in or management of different training options.

Table 6.3 *Example of staff development for school improvement plan*

Planned action with timescales	Who?	Resource implications	Success criteria	How will this be monitored and evaluated?
Induction programme for new teachers, including staff handbook revised by PDG (September training day)	Chair of PDG	Cost of refreshments. Cost of printing new staff handbook.	New staff have knowledge of: • school aims and values • main policies and key procedures • members of SLT and their responsibilities.	Monitored via evaluation questionnaires to staff. Evaluated by the chair of the PDG and the Head Teacher
Behaviour management skills (1) (November after-school meetings)	All of PDG	Some photocopying.	Staff who attend have had the opportunity to develop their skills and have identified one area of practice they are going to try to change.	(As above)
Behaviour management skills (2) Creating a positive classroom climate (February training day)	Chair and some of PDG	Cost of refreshments. Some photocopying costs.	All staff have had the opportunity to reflect on positive classroom climate and have identified at least one area for personal improvement.	(As above)

Professional Development Portfolios

All members of staff should be encouraged to keep a Professional Development Portfolio which they can update as they move through their careers. This helps to reinforce the notion of professional growth and reflection throughout a teaching career. Certificates given for attendance at training or being involved in the delivery of training can be kept in this portfolio as evidence of professional progress. This is particularly helpful for those planning to apply to cross the threshold. The Professional Development Portfolio can be a ring-binder with the following headings:

- Qualifications
- National Standards for Qualified Teacher Status: evidence
- Evidence of professional development
- Threshold standards: evidence.

Planning for group training

If the PDG decides to do some training within the group, for example on basic behaviour management techniques, the first requirement is to have a training plan. The plan identifies:

- what the training is about;
- who is involved;
- when it is happening;
- what activities are involved;
- the materials that are needed; and
- the timings of the activities.

It can also provide the 'script' for the training to keep the staff delivering the training 'on message'. (This is particularly helpful when teachers have little or no experience of training their peers.)

In writing the training plan, it will be important to plan for a variety of activities, take account of the learning styles of the group, and maintain pace and challenge. In training, the aim is to bring about a change in the practice of individuals in the group and this may mean a focus on activities which engage teachers actively and enable them to think through the issues and how they would react in a particular situation. The following approaches work well here:

- *Role play related to realistic scenarios*. Here members of the group act out different roles using prepared scripts or scenarios. Although some teachers are reluctant to begin with in this approach, it can result in significant learning gains because it enables participants to see situations from different perspectives. It can be particularly powerful if the role play takes place in a 'goldfish bowl' with other training participants sitting round the action and then discussing it afterwards.
- *Focused discussion* is discussion based on a preliminary activity which has enabled the participant to begin to think more deeply about an issue. It can follow on from role play or can focus on specific realistic written scenarios created to fit the topic.
- *Brainstorming* encourages group participation in an unthreatening and non-judgemental way. It can be an effective warm-up activity.
- *Visualising* requires teachers to visualise and draw a key focus of the training. It is often better to use this towards the end of the training when teachers have had a chance to explore their own thinking more fully. Pictures are often wonderfully insightful and humorous.
- Examination of personal practice.
- Commitment to small steps of change.

Point for reflection

Consider the following training plan and identify the extent to which the different activities planned actively engage teachers.

This is an example of staff training planned by a Professional Development Group for one of a series of whole-school training activities looking at the characteristics of an effective school. Here the focus was on creating positive teacher–pupil relationships and the aim was to bring about change in the way in which some teachers related negatively to pupils.

Title of training: Effective schools 1 – creating positive teacher–pupil relationships	**Date of training:** **Location of training:**
Aims of training: To enable staff to understand the nature and importance of positive teacher–pupil relationships and to reflect on their own beliefs and practice in this respect	**Staff involved in delivery of training:** 3 members of PDG **Training delivered to:** All staff
Resources required: OHP/PowerPoint (PP) facility	**Materials to be produced:** <ul><li>OHP/PP 1 – Characteristics of effective schools</li><li>Handout copy of this (40 copies)</li><li>Card sort activity based on beliefs about teacher–pupil relationships (20 sets)</li><li>OHP/PP 2 – Styles of managing pupils (rating activity)</li><li>OHP/PP 3 – 'Tough love'</li><li>Case study of a teacher–pupil relationship 1</li><li>Case study of a teacher–pupil relationship 2</li><li>Flip chart and felt tip pens</li><li>OHP/PP 4 – How teacher behaviour influences pupil behaviour</li></ul>

(Continued)

(Continued)

Activities: Aims and outline of the training	Trainer's script Explain that aim of training is to look briefly at the characteristics of effective schools and to focus in more detail on the nature of teacher–pupil relationships in these schools. Give brief overview of the training activities.
Characterstics of an effective school – OHP/PP 1 and handout	Comment briefly. Show OHP/PP slide of the list of effectiveness characteristics and give out handout copy of same with additional section for personal self-assessment. Ask staff to work in pairs to complete the handout, identifying two things that they currently do against the listed characteristics. Request brief oral/written feedback on this, emphasising the point that creating an effective school is something we all need to engage in. (10 mins).
Building positive relationships – case study 1 (focused discussion)	Work in pairs to identify the barriers to and opportunities for building positive teacher–pupil relationships in this classroom.
Your beliefs about the teacher–pupil relationship – card sort activity	Explain that individual relationships with students are based on personal beliefs about the teacher's role and the role of pupils. What you believe about this relationship also controls the kinds of strategies you use with students. Individually, do the card sort activity on a number of common beliefs and the teaching strategies related to them – choose 3 or 4 that you personally 'own'. Discuss with a partner.

(Continued)

(Continued)

Styles of managing pupils – OHP/PP 2	Brainstorm the kinds of responses which teachers using each of these styles of management are likely to elicit from pupils.
Rate yourself against the 'tough love' style – OHP/PP 3	Focus on 'tough love' management style and be explicit that this is the approach which will deliver positive teacher–pupil relationships and so this is the style all should aim for.
	Ask teachers to work in pairs to rate themselves on a scale of 0–10 on the extent to which their current practice matches the 'tough love' model.
	• How come they've chosen that number and not 0? • What do they already do that is successful? • What are the smallest things that they could and would do to increase their score by 1 point?
	Encourage whole-group feedback and discussion.
Visualising activity – pens and flip chart paper	Work in groups to visualise what an effective teacher who builds positive relationships with pupils looks like and draw them. Group feedback and discussion.
Case study 2 (focused discussion)	How can a positive relationship be built by the teacher of this class and the individuals in it? Discussion and feedback in groups or whole-group brainstorming activity (depending on time).

(Continued)

(Continued)

The teacher's role in creating relationship with pupils – OHP/PP 4	Reinforce message that what you do in your classroom has a real effect on pupils' behaviour and learning.

Because the aim of the training described above was to bring about change in the actual practice of some teachers, there was an emphasis on:

- **Personal practice and accountability** (i.e. what do I currently do in relation to this issue?). An example of a training material showing this approach is shown below.

Point for reflection	
Read the characteristics of an effective school and identify what you do in your own practice to contribute to each of these factors.	
Characteristics of an effective school	**What I do to promote/achieve this**
An ethos built on the belief that everyone is valued	
A recognition by pupils that staff treat them fairly and are committed to teaching them	
Effective and consistent routines	
A concern that pupils feel secure in terms of both the physical environment and emotionally	
Strategies for making learning dynamic, interesting and challenging	

(Continued)   **109**

(Continued)

A clear partnership between school, pupils and parents	
Displays which support learning and celebrate success	
Latest HMCI report (Ofsted)	

- **Realistic rather than theoretical case studies.** Writing these can be an imaginative and often humorous activity for the PDG. Two further examples of case study or scenario writing are given below:

Point for reflection

Read the following case studies and identify the barriers to and the opportunities for a positive teacher–pupil relationship in each of these classrooms.

Case study 1

This is the group from hell! They burst into your room like the Visigoths on an away-day. They run round the room, fighting and spitting at each other. They totally ignore you when you scream at them to be quiet. Eventually, exhausted, they slump into their seats and you attempt to write the learning objectives on the board. While your back is turned, Marlon biffs Casey and Casey runs out of the room in tears. You leave the room to console Casey as the Teaching Assistant (TA) arrives. You ask the TA to quell the riot. The TA gives all the pupils pencils and paper and persuades them to write down the lesson objectives. You ask the pupils to copy a passage out of the book in the hope that this will settle them down but Marlon who can't read soon tires of this and starts an argument with Sean. This is much more interesting for the rest of the class than copying from a book and they are soon distracted. You shout at Marlon and send him out of the room and try to move the rest of the class onto the next activity. Marlon keeps opening the door trying to get back in and disrupting the lesson, then he trips up Casey who is also still out of the room. You detach the TA from the quiet girl she is helping in the corner of the room and dispatch her to sort out Marlon and Casey. This takes the rest of the

---

(Continued)

lesson. At the end of the lesson, Sean screws up the piece of paper he has been writing on and throws it in the bin, announcing loudly that 'this is crap!' You are at the end of your tether and the Head Teacher wants you to establish a positive relationship with these animals!

Case study 2

You teach a Year 9 Higher set for four periods: two periods in mornings and one period 4 and the other period 5. In the period 5 lesson, the class, which is a large one with a higher proportion of boys, is often restless and unco-operative. Several of them regularly come late having stopped for a cigarette break on the way. You are often late yourself to this lesson because you teach one period of PE period 4 and it is a rush getting changed and back up from the gym on time. You try to start your lessons with calling registration but this is often interrupted by latecomers who fling the door open and make a dramatic entrance. Two of the boys in particular are troublemakers who interact with each other throughout the lesson and distract themselves and others. You are concerned about one of the weaker girls in the class who you feel is being bullied by some of the other girls. You try to help this girl in the lesson, giving her a lot of attention to try to boost her self-esteem. The end of the lesson is often a rush because of the delayed start of the lesson and pupils do not always write their homework down properly and some of them regularly come to the lesson without books let alone homework. It's all feeling like an uphill battle and then the Head Teacher expects you to develop a positive relationship with these pupils!

- **Examining underlying beliefs which control actions.** One successful way of doing this is to do an individual card sort activity based on personal beliefs about particular situations. The example below relates to the training plan set out above and was designed to help teachers to think through their beliefs about their relationships with pupils.

Point for reflection

Card sort activity – teachers' beliefs

Children have to be controlled	'Don't smile until Christmas' is good advice

(Continued)

(Continued)

Children should do as they are told	Most children know how to behave well
Many children don't know how to behave	Many children don't know how to behave and teachers have to teach them this
Children should respect adults	If one person gets away with it, they'll all do it
Rules need to be strictly enforced	Rules need to be constantly explained and reinforced
The teacher has to win when there is a battle of wills in the classroom	Children need nurturing like buds on a flower.
It is important for children to like their teacher	Being nice and friendly makes children like you
Misbehaviour must be confronted immediately	It is important to negotiate their learning with pupils
Sharing confidences with pupils makes them think of you as a human being	Planning good work and differentiating prevents human misbehaviour
It is important to listen to pupils' problems so that they can turn to you when they need help	A teacher needs to set clear boundaries
Children will always test the boundaries adults set	Some children are deliberately disruptive
Children making mistakes about their behaviour is normal	Teachers need to teach behaviour and social skills as well as subjects
Children should be helped to experience achievement	Caring means saying 'No' and meaning it at the right time
It's the job of parents to teach behaviour and social skills – teachers should not do this	When a child misbehaves in a lesson it is always the fault of the child

(Continued)

(Continued)

When a child misbehaves in a lesson it is sometimes the fault of the teacher	Management must always back up the teacher when a child misbehaves
There is always more to a child than the problems s/he presents	With workforce remodelling, teachers should just concentrate on teaching and should not have to be involved in behaviour management

- Being explicit about the direction the school is intending to go in and the values and research on which this direction is based.
- Visualising effective practice.
- Building consensus around the desired approach.

Point for reflection

Consider the advantages and disadvantages of the following training. The materials written for this training consisted of two roles and a letter and the training was devised by a Professional Development Group to meet the needs identified by some members of the group to improve their management of difficult situations with parents. Here all of the group were given the letter from the parent, then two experienced members of the group played the role of the parent and the role of the pastoral head using the case study information given. The rest of the group acted as observers for the role play and were asked to focus, in particular, on how body language and the choice of words spoken added to, or helped to resolve, the conflict. All were then involved in a focused discussion about what they had seen. At the end of the session, group members were asked to brainstorm issues that could have been dealt with differently to provide a positive resolution to the incident.

(Continued)

(Continued)

Letter from parent

Dear teacher,

My son Shane tells me that you have been picking on him yet again for no reason. Shane is a sensitive boy who needs nurturing not you shouting at him the whole time just because the dog ate his homework and he tried to explain but no one would listen. You are always upsetting my son and my son's friends tell me you can't keep the class in order so how do you expect the boy to do his homework anyway? I am going to contact the governors about your bullying behaviour, shouting at my son and upsetting him and I can tell you now that my son will not be attending no after-school detention tomorrow night. NO WAY.
Signed
Mrs I. M. Angry

Role play 1: Pastoral head

You were late into school today because the car wouldn't start at first, and you know that you must ring the garage to book it in as soon as possible. You have a full teaching load and you are mentoring pupils on the C/D borderline at lunchtime. You have already missed seeing the six pupils on report who you see daily, and when you get in there are already three referrals from the previous day on your desk. In each case staff have referred pupils but have not indicated that they are taking any initial action. As you rush to your class – 11(6) again – the LSA assigned to this class runs after you to say that there is a parent in reception demanding to see you about a detention. The parent is very angry and the office staff want you to see her immediately because she is shouting and causing a disturbance in the office. You know it is important for you to uphold the school's policy on detentions.

Role play 2: The parent

You have had a difficult time since you split up with Shane's step dad. You have had to move further away from school and it is not easy to get Shane to the school. You want to keep him at the school because it is a good school but you also have to get his younger

---

(Continued)

(Continued)

brother to a different school and get to work in the supermarket by 8.45 a.m. The boys have been very unsettled since the split and have taken to hanging round with older boys on the estate in the evening. Some of the neighbours say they are up to no good. You are often exhausted by the time you get in, and Shane and his brother quarrel a lot. Shane has been asking if he can go and live with his real dad in the city and this has upset you because Shane's dad used to knock you about. Money is tight and you cannot always give the boys the things you want and sometimes you feel at the end of your tether trying to keep things going on your own. Now the school is sending you stupid letters about detentions for not doing homework and Shane burst into tears when you shouted at him for the letter and said he hated you. If Shane is kept after school, you won't have time to collect him and his younger brother from the other school and give them their tea before you go back to the supermarket for the shelf-stacking shift in the late evening. Anyway, what good is French to a boy in this area? These teachers with their stupid letters don't know what the real world is all about, and Shane is not going to do any detention.

This approach had the following advantages:

- it was designed to meet a particular expressed need;
- it focused on a real-life scenario which teachers had encountered or were likely to;
- it encouraged group members to discuss different responses and thus extended their repertoire of possible approaches;
- it encouraged group members to 'see' the impact of body language and use of language in a behavioural context; and
- it built group commitment to good practice.

The kind of training which the PDG can get involved in will depend upon the skills of the chair person as well as the willingness of the group to engage actively with the process of training themselves and others. However, the right approach could build a powerful model of continuing professional development and professional growth within the school, maintaining and promoting teacher effectiveness and helping the whole school to continue to improve and adapt in an ever-changing world.

Recruiting and selecting effective teachers

Normally, it is a school's senior leaders that participate in the recruitment and selection of staff. Together with members of the governing body, they invest a great deal of time in the process because they know the importance of making the right appointment. It follows that securing the right appointment now will greatly reduce the need to tackle under-performance in the future. Increasingly, however, other line-managers are being used to support the process, partly because of their specialist knowledge of particular curriculum areas, but also to ensure a balance of appropriate skills and attributes within the teams they lead, e.g. key stage, pastoral. This chapter has *not* been written for those who are already highly experienced in recruitment and selection processes (although there may be some helpful ideas) but for those, such as middle leaders, who may find themselves undertaking such responsibilities for the first time or in the future.

Selecting an effective teacher can make a significant difference, not only to the subject or area they teach in, but also to the school's overall improvement. Highly effective teachers are models of the professionalism and commitment expected in a modern teaching profession. Such teachers can act as mentors and guides for younger staff and can develop and hone their skills by becoming involved in whole-school professional development. They are a precious resource for school leaders and need to be both recruited carefully and given every opportunity to develop professionally.

Being systematic

It is important to have a systematic approach to recruitment in order to:

- ensure that you get the best possible field from which to fill the vacancy;
- meet the requirements of employment and equal opportunities legislation;

- ensure that everyone involved in the recruitment and selection process has a positive view of the school, whether or not an appointment is made; and
- ensure that the right decision is made at the end of the process.

One of the first decisions to make is whether you actually need to make an appointment. In some circumstances, it may be fairly obvious that a vacancy has to be filled, but in others, it may be useful to check the school's future curriculum needs and surpluses before deciding that a vacancy actually exists. If a new appointment is contemplated, before going ahead, school leaders need to be clear about two key matters:

- the purpose of that post; and
- how the post fits into the school's improvement plan.

Getting the timing right

The timing of any recruitment is also important. If you have a vacancy to fill for the forthcoming year, and advertise in June, the field of potential applicants is usually thinner than in September or October, or by February and March when new entrants finishing their PGCE training are becoming available. It is important to weigh up the advantages and disadvantages of appointing a temporary member of staff for a term or a year and doing your recruitment for the post at the optimum time for getting a strong field, against the unsettling effect of a temporary appointment. This is a decision that needs to be taken at the relevant time, in light of the strengths and weaknesses of a particular subject area and of the school's improvement plans.

Point for reflection

Consider the situation of the school described below and decide:

- whether an appointment needs to be made at all;
- whether it should be full or part time;
- whether a permanent appointment needs to be made immediately; or
- whether a temporary member of staff should be recruited for a term or a year.

The school's only German teacher obtained a new appointment on the last day of May (traditionally the last available day for handing in notice for starting a new job in September). She was

---

(Continued)

(Continued)

> an experienced teacher with four GCSE exam classes in Year 10 and two GCSE exam classes due to start in September. There is an existing curriculum surplus of 23 periods per week in the Languages Department, spread between two part timers who teach French and have Spanish not German as their second language. The school has plans to develop a specialism in business studies and would like to be able to offer Spanish, not German, as its second language linked to a business studies qualification. Parents of pupils currently in the middle of their German GCSE have contacted the school to express their concerns about issues of continuity for these pupils who tend to be the most able pupils in the school.

Advertising for maximum impact

Having decided that a full-time, permanent member of staff is required, thought now needs to be given to the advertisement of the post. The teaching press has hundreds of advertisements for posts every week and some school leaders – rightly or wrongly – take the view that the bigger and bolder the advertisement, the more likely it is to attract attention. Others feel that the majority of applicants tend to be locally based and emphasise the location of the school or its accessibility. As a minimum, an advertisement should normally provide the following information:

- Whether the post is permanent or temporary (and the duration of a temporary appointment).
- The pay rate (as Teaching and Learning Responsibility (TLR) payments are spot payments which will vary from school to school for similar posts, it will be important to specify the actual amount).
- The type of school (e.g. junior, mixed comprehensive, middle deemed secondary).
- The location of the school put in positive terms (e.g. 'semi-rural location' will sound better than 'on the edge of the city').
- A brief, positive comment about the school (e.g. 'identified by Ofsted as an improving school' or 'winner of the curriculum award for . . . ', etc.).
- The name of the head teacher.
- The full postal address of the school.
- The name of the person to be contacted about the vacancy together with phone, fax and e-mail contact details.
- The closing date for applications.

Whatever your approach, you will want to maximise the number of people who see the advertisement so that you can get the best possible field from which to fill your vacancy. This might mean:

- placing a large advertisement in the teaching press (in colour even!);
- placing adverts in the local press covering a 20- to 40-mile radius of the school;
- contacting all the local and regional PGCE providers and asking them to put your advertisement on the student e-mail system;
- maintaining regular contacts with PGCE course organisers (many schools act as placement providers for PGCE courses, so that they have good links with the sources of new entrants to the profession and can 'have a look' at potential recruits while they are in training);
- telling your own workforce of the vacancy (word of mouth is a powerful means of communication); and
- speaking to supply agencies to see if they have anyone on their books who may be looking for permanent employment at some point.

It is worth putting considerable energy and commitment into this early stage of recruitment. Without a good field of applicants, the prospect of making a high quality appointment diminishes significantly.

Information for applicants

The next stage of the recruitment process is to consider the written material you are going to send to those who enquire about the vacancy. At this stage, you should consider carefully the nature of the person you wish to recruit and draw up a list of 'desirable' and 'essential' requirements. These criteria will form the basis for the person specification for the post. In doing so, you will need to reflect on the existing subject area team, especially their strengths, weaknesses and complementary skills. A matrix, similar to the one in Table 7.1, can be used to aid reflection and analysis.

Defining the post

You will also need to consider the requirements of the post itself, e.g. ability to work with a range of external agencies, high-level interpersonal skills. If you are seeking to recruit an effective teacher, you are likely to want candidates who can exhibit:

- good written and oral communication skills;
- self-confidence;
- good curriculum and subject knowledge;
- an ability to plan and structure lessons appropriately;

Table 7.1   *Team analysis matrix*

Curriculum area leader	Teacher 1	Teacher 2	Vacancy
Strengths:	Strengths:	Strengths:	
Weaknesses:	Weaknesses:	Weaknesses:	

Conclusion: What sort of person does this team need?

- a knowledge of pupils' special educational needs (SEN) and how to adapt lesson planning to these needs;
- good interpersonal skills;
- an understanding of assessment practice and how it can promote learning;
- a willingness to seek and take advice;
- good judgement; and
- additional skills or strengths.

You may want to specify the level of qualification or experience required, e.g. upper second-class degree or better, or one to five years' prior experience of teaching. This 'paragon' will also require persistence, energy, commitment and all the other qualities you feel are desirable in your ideal candidate.

As you start to list these attributes, begin also to think about how you will find out, in the short time you have with individual candidates, whether or not they possess these desirable attributes. For example, how will you make use of the application form, the references, the letter or the interview process itself to answer the different aspects of this question? Some suggestions are provided in Table 7.2.

While you are doing that exercise, it is worth checking that:

- the application form you are using asks for the necessary information;
- the accompanying letter written by candidates will provide the relevant information; and
- the interview process will be structured to enable you to gather the relevant information.

Table 7.2   *Testing for desirable attributes in applicants*

Desirable attributes	How tested?
• Good written and oral communication skills	Letter/Application form
• Self-confidence	Interview
• Good curriculum or subject knowledge	Letter/References/Interview
• An ability to plan and structure lessons appropriately	References/Interview
• A knowledge of pupils' SEN and how to adapt lesson planning to these needs	Letter/Interview
• Good interpersonal skills	Interview
• An understanding of assessment practice and how it can promote learning	Interview
• A willingness to seek and take advice	Interview
• Good judgement	Interview
• Additional skills or strengths which the individual can bring to the team	Letter/Application form
• An upper second-class degree or better from a recognised university	Application form
• PGCE or alternative teaching qualification	Application form
• Some experience of teaching	Application form

Person specification

At the end of this period of analysis and reflection, you will need to devise a person specification, similar to the one shown in Table 7.3. Here you may wish to divide the attributes you are looking for into ones that are 'desirable' and those that are 'essential' for the post.

You will need to send this person specification to applicants, with the job details, and will want to use it when you are short-listing candidates to call for interview.

Job descriptions

It is helpful to look at the existing job description even if the intention is merely to replace an existing member of staff. The school's situation changes from year to year and it may be important to update the job description to incorporate different requirements (although it is important to note that this may mean updating the job descriptions of other teachers employed for a post with the same name and same remuneration, which may lead to an end-of - year staff restructuring exercise rather than just playing around with a few words or sentences).

If a totally new post is called for, thought needs to be given to the:

- purpose of the job (how will this new job help the school achieve its improvement objectives?);
- scope of the job (who and what is the postholder responsible for?);

Table 7.3   *Example of a person specification*

Attributes	Desirable	Essential
• Good written and oral communication skills		✓
• Self-confidence	✓	
• Good curriculum or subject knowledge		✓
• An ability to plan and structure lessons appropriately		✓
• A knowledge of pupils' SEN and how to adapt lesson planning to these needs	✓	
• Good interpersonal skills	✓	
• An understanding of assessment practice and how it can promote learning	✓	
• A willingness to seek and take advice	✓	
• Good judgement		✓
• Additional skills or strengths which the individual can bring to the team	✓	
• An upper second-class degree or better from a recognised university	✓	
• PGCE or alternative teaching qualification		✓
• Some experience of teaching		✓

- accountabilities of the job (what is the postholder accountable for and to whom?);
- main features of the job (a broad outline, rather than a detailed list).

(Figure 7.1) is an example of a job description for a new post: Director of Teaching and Learning in a small secondary school.

Details sent to applicants

The next stage of the recruitment process is to consider the written material you are going to send to those who enquire about the vacancy. You need to send the job specification and the person specification but you might also want to send out some information about the school and about the area to which you are recruiting. Badly photocopied sections from an out-of-date staff handbook may not create the most favourable impression, and it is worth spending some time looking at the material you are going to send to ensure that it conveys the impression that your school is the place where the best candidates will want to work. Even if they decide that they don't want to work in your school, they may have children whom they are considering sending to your school and it is important not to lose any potential marketing opportunity.

Job details

Job title: Director of Teaching and Learning (Science/PE) TLR 1a £6,500
Reports to: Assistant Head Teacher (line-manager) and responsible to the Head Teacher
in all matters
Date: June 2005

Purpose:
To provide professional leadership and management of the staff in the designated curriculum group in order to secure high quality teaching, the effective use of resources and improving standards of learning and achievement for all students.

Dimensions:

- Students:
- Staff:7 teaching staff, 2 technicians
- Capitation: £7,430

Principal accountabilities:
Strategic planning:

1. To act as subject leader for own subject (see job description).
2. To ensure there is a development plan for the curriculum group which will allow the school's aims to be fulfilled, using the school's development plan and up-to-date curriculum knowledge.
3. To support good discipline in the curriculum group, adhering to the whole-school behaviour policy and liaising with the key stage managers to control the behaviour of pupils effectively.
4. To be a member of the Teaching and Learning Steering Group, and to act as chair, working with senior managers to secure high quality teaching and learning throughout the school.

Accountability for leading, managing and developing the curriculum group

1. Co-ordinate strategies to achieve relevant school improvement priorities that have been identified in the school development plan.
2. Evaluate and report on the effectiveness of practice in the curriculum group annually, suggesting areas and issues for further improvement.
3. Lead professional development in the faculty through example and support and co-ordinate the provision of high quality professional development for staff.
4. Build effective links with the local community, including business and industry, in order to develop work-related learning.
5. Use financial and resource management innovatively and effectively.

Impact on educational progress beyond assigned pupils

1. Monitor and evaluate assessment data across the curriculum group to identify trends in pupil performance and issues for development. Liaise with key stage managers where individual pupil under-performance is an issue.
2. Evaluate and report on the effectiveness of intervention strategies identified in the subject development plans.

(Continued)

Figure 7.1 *Job description for Director of Teaching and Learning*

Figure 7.1 *(Continued)*

---

3. Identify performance management objectives with staff, including quantifiable and challenging pupil progress objectives.
4. Support teachers in planning appropriate strategies to ensure pupils achieve their targets.

Leading, developing and enhancing the teaching practice of others

1. Monitor and evaluate the planning of teachers in the curriculum group, providing constructive and development feedback on a regular basis.
2. Disseminate examples of good practice within the curriculum group and share these within curriculum group and across the school.
3. Ensure the feedback from lesson observation, work scrutiny and analysis of assessment data is appropriately reflected in teachers' planning.
4. Observe colleagues teaching (through performance management arrangements and subject monitoring) and provide evaluative feedback on the effectiveness of their teaching strategies to bring about further improvement.
5. Identify and promote innovative and effective teaching strategies in the curriculum group to meet the needs of all pupils, and in response to government and LEA initiatives.
6. Co-ordinate and monitor the deployment of teachers, support staff and other adults to ensure their effective contribution to pupils' learning.

You could consider sending:

- the school prospectus;
- the most recent newsletter to parents (to give a broader picture of all the activities happening in your school);
- leaflets (not too many) about relevant aspects of your school, e.g. special needs provision;
- the school's teaching and learning policy; and
- the section from the most recent Ofsted inspection report which relates to the curriculum, subject or year relevant to the vacancy.

The letter of application

It is common practice to ask applicants to write a covering letter with the standard job application. Here, you may need to refer back to the list of personal attributes and how you are going to test whether or not applicants demonstrate these. For example, if 'imagination' and 'creativity' are important attributes for the post, you may ask candidates to write a letter in which they make it clear how they will make their subject and their teaching interesting and varied for pupils of all abilities.

Record of contact						
Post: _____						
Advertised: (date)		Closing date:		Interview date:		
Contact name and address	Who took message?	Phone/Fax no(s): e-mail:		Date of contact	Information sent (date)	Where advert seen?

Figure 7.2 *Record of contact with applicants*

Organising the responses from applicants

Ensure that staff supporting the administration of the appointment process have complete sets of the job information literature and application forms to send out in response to enquiries. It is also helpful to keep a record of the names and contact details of potential applicants who ring up asking for details, including the date and method of contact (Figure 7.2). If you fail to recruit for the post, you may need to speak to these potential applicants to find out why they did not proceed with an application.

Short-listing applicants

Once received, analyse the application forms and letters and undertake a formal short-listing process, preferably involving several colleagues in order to minimise individual bias. It is helpful to have a conversation with these colleagues before you start the short-listing so that any implicit bias can be examined and resolved. For example, some colleagues may have implicit biases for or against handwritten or word-processed applications. Rules of fairness would dictate that if the school has not specified either handwriting or word processing, then either approach must be equally acceptable. Obviously candidates cannot be discriminated against on the basis of age, gender, race or disability and it is important to be explicit about this with the short-listing group. Even if there are only relatively few applicants, it is important to go through a systematic, and demonstrably fair, short-listing process. This will save you trouble in the future if a

Table 7.4 *Summary of candidates' information*

Name	Address/contact details	Qualifications post 16 (with dates)	Previous experience (with dates)	Reference details
Jane Murphy	24 The Smithy Stoke on Trent ST17 OHT Tel: E-mail:	• A levels: Maths D; Geography E; Art D (1990); English C (1991) • BA Hons in Geography Cardiff University class 2:2 (1994) • PGCE Cardiff (1995)	Shop work (1988–90) Bar work (1992–3) Class teacher Housedale Primary (1995–6) Class teacher Armford First School (1996–7) Class teacher Peasley First School (1997–ongoing)	Head Teacher Peasley First School Tel: PGCE tutor Cardiff Tel:
John Vernon	9 Forge Cottage Presley Oxford OX7 DB8 Tel: Email:	• A levels: Geography B; History B; English B (1999) • BA in Humanities London University class 2:1 (2002) • PGCE London (2003)	Class teacher Hackend Junior (2003–4) Insurance clerk (2004–5) Hackend Junior (2005–ongoing)	PGCE tutor London Tel: Head Teacher Hackend Junior Tel:
Betsy Carter	42 Bleaford Common Scamley SC8 4DR Tel: E-mail:	• A levels: Geography E; History B; Psychology E (2001) • BA Hons Child Development Studies and Geography Hull (2004) • PGCE Hull started (2004)	Bar work 2001–4 First placement: Mondem C of E Primary school (2004) Second placement: Flaherty First School (2005)	PGCE tutor Hull Tel: Professional tutor Mondem C of E Primary School Tel:

potential candidate queries your decisions. Where there are many candidates, it is the only way of managing the wide range of information provided by applicants.

Initial analysis can provide a quick summary of the personal details of applicants and is helpful later when you want to fully understand the academic, training and career history of applicants. The example in Table 7.4 sets out a way in which a summary of candidates' details might be organised.

Point for reflection

Study the summary details in Table 7.4 and record the thoughts you have about each applicant and their academic, training and career history.

- Where are the gaps in the details?
- What points might you want to explore further with the candidate?
- Have you made any implicit assumptions about any candidate (e.g. that the first candidate may be lacking in commitment because she has had a number of jobs in a short space of time)? (In fact, the candidate had struggled to find permanent employment and had done several maternity leave covers – hence the change in jobs.)

The initial analysis is a helpful summary to have to hand throughout the short-listing and interviewing process. You will need a different form for the actual short-listing process to allow you to relate to the attributes you have identified for this post. In the post for an effective main scale teacher described above, seven attributes have been specified which are to be judged from the application form and letter of application. You will need to decide whether to seek references first and, if so, you should include these in your short-listing process. However, in practice, it can take time to get these references and because some of your candidates for short-listing will have them and some will not, it may be fairer to save consideration of references until you get to the point of interviewing.

Short-listing using a grid like the one in Table 7.5 can be time consuming although it is not necessary to record decisions and information in the same detail as given in this example. However, it is time well spent if it helps you to select the best candidate to fill your vacancy. Recording the reasons for not selecting some individuals and having a clear set of criteria for short-listing against will also protect you from any later claims of bias or unfairness.

In practice, you are often not comparing like with like when you are short-listing. For example, you may have to weigh up the relative advantages of a bright youngster straight out of college, with very limited experience but with lots of enthusiasm, against the proven skills of a more mature and experienced candidate whose qualifications are not as good. Here, the exercise earlier to identify the kind of person best suited to the team in which the vacancy exists

Table 7.5 *Summarising key facts about applicants*

Name	Written skills	Knowledge of SEN	Additional skills/areas/ qualities	Degree and class	PGCE or other	Experience	Notes	Reasons for short-listing/rejecting
Candidate 1	No spelling/ grammatical errors. Correct use of paragraphing and punctuation. Writing fluent and meaning clear.	Has had Dyslexia Institute training.	Qualified football coach. Willing to run after school teams.	BA Geography (2:1) Hull University.	PGCE with commendation in teaching practice.	Two years' teaching experience (maternity leave cover) in two different schools.	Looks strong candidate on paper.	Short-listed – meets all criteria for short-listing and has additional skill to offer plus commendation in her teaching practice indicating that she is likely to be a strong teacher.
Candidate 2	No spelling errors. Some grammatical lapses. Paragraphing spasmodic but meaning generally clear.	Not mentioned.	Has organised field trip during teaching practice and keen on applied studies.	BA Geography (3rd Class) Open University.	Graduate teacher training scheme with LEA.	Teaching practice placements in two schools.		Not short-listed – does not meet qualification criterion which was considered essential to the post. No information given about SEN which was a desirable attribute for the post.
Candidate 3	No spelling/ grammatical errors. Correct use of paragraphing and punctuation. Meaning clear.	Attended several SEN courses including dyslexia, dyspraxia and autism.	Experience as an LSA has given her a good understanding of teaching and learning and behaviour management techniques.	BA Child Development Studies (2:1) London University.	PGCE.	5 years' experience in schools as an LSA. Teaching practice placements in two schools.		Short-listed – meets basic criteria and although her experience as a teacher is limited, she has 5 years' experience as an LSA.

will be helpful. A team that already has weaknesses may not be the best place to nurture and develop a new entrant, and here a higher priority or weighting can be given to 'experience' in the short-listing process.

How many to short-list?

During barren periods of recruitment into teaching, this is an easy question to answer. Where there are only a few candidates, you are likely to short-list most of them because you want to give yourself the widest possible choice in a difficult situation. In most circumstances, it is sensible to short-list no more than 6–8 candidates because the logistics of interviewing so many, especially if you want to see them teach, become unmanageable. However, you may wish to short-list up to 8 candidates at the height of the recruitment period (usually April – May), as you will often find that short-listed candidates may have found employment elsewhere. If you find yourself with 6 or 8 candidates on the day of the interview, be prepared to make a 'cut' at lunchtime so that you take no more than 4 candidates through to the formal interview process in the afternoon.

The selection process

Running an effective interview process is physically and mentally demanding on the day, and you will want to get the groundwork correct beforehand. Be clear about your own approach to the interview process. Some colleagues take a 'survival of the fittest' approach to the process, setting a series of potentially frightening hurdles and tasks that individual candidates have to surmount and survive during the course of the day. This approach may be relevant if you are seeking to appoint a head teacher or senior leader who will need to be 'steady under fire'. However, the approach taken in this book is one which acknowledges that candidates will be nervous anyway and should be treated courteously and fairly if they are to be seen performing as well as they can, i.e. catching them being good rather than catching them out. The final interview may be the place for probing questions that put an individual on the spot, but it hardly seems necessary to do this at the outset of the process. Whether appointed or not, it is important for candidates to have a positive view of your school as a place where individuals are valued and treated courteously.

When you have decided on your approach, map out the planned day with timings. A common interview process format is to see candidates teaching a specified group, followed by discussions with relevant team leaders and others. These activities are usually followed by a more formal interview with school governors. Often, a tour of the school is also included which provides not only

08.45–09.00	Welcome and introductions
09.00–10.30	Teaching observation with Class 1. Please prepare a 25-minute lesson on a topic of your choice. If you require additional equipment, e.g. OHP/PP, please contact Mrs Evans on (tel. no.) to arrange prior to the day
10.30–10.45	Coffee in the staff-room
10.45–11.15	Tour of the school
11.45–12.30	Professional discussions with Key Stage 1 Co-ordinator and Deputy Head
12.30–13.15	Lunch with Key Stage 1 team
13.15–15.30	Formal interviews with governors and Head Teacher

Figure 7.3 *A possible time-table for the selection process*

an opportunity for the candidates to see if they like the school, but also an additional and less formal opportunity to assess candidates' social and personal skills. Sometimes the task of leading the school tour is delegated to pupils who are later asked for their views on the candidates. Other schools may include lunch with the designated team members as a further opportunity for informal assessment. So, a plan for the interview process might look similar to the one shown in Figure 7.3.

Invitation to short-listed candidates to attend the interview

As part of the preparation for the interview process, short-listed candidates will need a letter telling them the day and time of the interviews. If you are inviting candidates from across the country, it is courteous to provide them with details of local accommodation, as they may want to travel the evening before, rather than having to risk a long journey on the morning of the interview process. Remember also to write to unsuccessful applicants informing them of your decision.

Creating the right impression for candidates

If you are the person welcoming candidates to the school, ensure that you:

- learn candidates' first names from the paperwork and some small individual detail (where they live, the school they are currently working at, an unusual hobby mentioned in their details) so that your welcome can be personal. This can help to make individuals feel valued (even if you don't subsequently appoint them) and help them to relax;

- introduce key people in the interview process by name, with their title or responsibilities, so that candidates are clear about whom they will be speaking to;
- provide candidates with a waiting room (possibly the staff-room) that is tidy, has refreshments, and is close to toilet facilities;
- invite particular staff to drop in during the course of the day to have a chat with candidates. This is, of course, a further informal assessment, and can help to make the candidates feel valued and welcomed. Teaching Assistants are often very good in this role;
- provide all candidates with a written outline of the day;
- invite candidates to have a look round the school when they are not being interviewed;
- check at the earliest opportunity whether candidates require any resources or equipment that they have not asked for, and have someone on hand who can arrange this quickly, if necessary;
- let candidates have a brief look at the classroom where they are going to teach their lesson; and
- have a team of reliable pupils who can support certain activities during the day.

Lesson observation

If you have decided to see candidates teaching (and it is strongly recommended that you do), you will need to:

- place the teaching observation at the beginning of the process as candidates may be nervous and unlikely to focus fully on other matters until they have done this;
- give details of the class candidates will be teaching and the level of ability of the class. It is usually enough of an ordeal for candidates to teach an unknown class for a short space of time with an observer present, let alone inflict on them a challenging class;
- be precise about the information given to candidates in the letter inviting them for interview and asking them to prepare a lesson. For example, 'middle-ability group' can mean different things in different contexts;
- be clear about the length of the lesson and whether it is a topic of the individual's choice or a topic chosen by you. (Observing different candidates' approach to the same topic can be helpful when comparisons about planning and preparation are being made later. This can help to avoid the situation where young trainee teachers resort to the one tried and tested lesson that their tutor has shown them and they know works in most situations);
- ensure that candidates know who to contact about additional resources or equipment otherwise you can find your carefully timed day soon upset by the need to locate resources and get them into the right room before the teaching starts;

- check the room(s) being used for teaching observation prior to the day so that any problems (not enough chairs, no board rubber, etc.) can be rectified;
- inform the candidates that the observer will bring the lesson to a conclusion if it over-runs its allotted time. This is to ensure that all candidates have the same amount of time and to keep the overall interview process schedule on time.

In your planning for the lesson observations, it is better to have two observers in the room; this will allow them to compare notes afterwards. However, in smaller schools, or with a large field of candidates, this may be difficult. All observers should, however, have a preliminary discussion about what an effective lesson might look like and, for consistency, should use the same observation schedule.

At the end of the lesson observation, observers should ensure that they have been given a copy of the lesson plan, thank the candidate and the class and send/escort the candidate back to the waiting room promptly so that the overall schedule keeps to time. A refreshment break in the staff-room is a good opportunity for candidates to meet a wider cross-section of the staff who work in the school. This helps candidates to get a feel for the school's culture and to sense whether they would like to work in this school. The interview process is a two-way process in which:

- the candidates decide whether they would like to work in this school; and
- the school decides which of these candidates best fits the vacancy.

Tour of the school

The tour of the school should continue the process of helping candidates to feel that they would like to work in this school. It is better to take candidates into a few classrooms and give them the opportunity to see work in progress than to walk the corridors giving them the history of the school's building improvements. In classrooms with pupils hard at work, candidates can begin to visualise how they themselves would work in this environment. Ensure that you:

- plan your route in advance;
- notify the relevant staff of the visit and that you would like them to continue teaching when the candidates come into the room; and
- encourage candidates to speak to individual pupils about their work as they circulate.

Encouraging discussion

Professional discussions are preliminary, semi-formal exchanges where the school can clarify aspects of the candidates' history and ideas provided in the letter and the application form. They also provide opportunities for candidates to ask questions in order to clarify the nature of the post and its requirements. For these reasons, it is important that:

- the candidates understand the purpose of the professional discussions;
- two people are involved in the professional discussions, one of whom is the team leader overseeing the post in question and who can answer detailed questions;
- anything that is not clear about a candidate's qualifications, academic record, training and employment history is clarified;
- candidates are given the opportunity to elaborate on their suitability for the post;
- at the end of the interview, each candidate is asked whether s/he is a firm applicant for the post (this is particularly important if you are about to shed some candidates from a field of 6–8 candidates); and
- most of the talking in these discussions is done by the candidate.

Lunch and the 'first cut'

Lunch with members of the team where the vacancy exists can provide them with a sense of involvement in the selection of their new colleague as well as giving candidates a sense of what it would be like to work in the team. Team leaders should be encouraged to 'brief' members of the team beforehand so that each candidate is given an equal opportunity to ask questions and to clarify his/her ideas. Although lunch can be a daunting social situation (asking questions, assessing potential new colleagues, thinking about the interview process and trying to eat politely, all at the same time), it can reinforce the individual's sense of being valued and being of interest to the group and the school.

While lunch is going on, the person running the interview process will want to confer with those who have been involved in the lesson observation and the professional discussions. If there are more than four candidates, consideration should now be given to a 'first cut' selection of candidates who will not go through into the final interview. The reasons for having a 'first cut' are as follows:

- Formal interviewing is a mentally demanding task and four candidates is the maximum that most formal interview panels can manage fairly and thoroughly in an afternoon.
- If your interview process has worked effectively so far, you should already have an idea of which candidates are unlikely to meet your standards and requirements.

Remember that the over-riding aim here is to appoint a highly effective and, hopefully, exceptional teacher. The right individual will make a significant difference to the area of the school into which s/he is placed and will help the school to move forward on its improvement agenda. Even if you have a poor

Table 7.6 *Key questions to help with the 'first cut'*

Name of candidate:	
Key questions for 'first cut'	**Yes/No**

- Was the teaching seen at least 'good', judged against Ofsted criteria for good teaching?
- Was the lesson planning and organisation 'good'?
- Were pupils responsive and did they make good progress?
- Has the candidate demonstrated good interpersonal skills in contacts with pupils and staff?
- Was there any aspect of the candidate's personal history/information/teaching/planning and organisation which made them a weaker candidate than others? If so, what?

(Think carefully about the response here. It may be that all the candidates have equally good grades for the first four questions, and you now need an objective reason to select out some candidates, e.g. lower qualifications, less experience, etc. Be vigilant about choosing items which unintentionally discriminate, for instance, against women who have had career breaks for family reasons.)

field, do not compromise on the question of teaching quality. Candidates are likely to perform as well as they can and if in this situation there is something lacking in their performance, you may regret taking them forward to the final interview.

Do not be tempted to make an appointment if you lack a suitable candidate, however strong the 'get a body in front of the class' argument is. An unsatisfactory appointment will cost you and your colleagues untold additional work in the future in attempting to recctify under-performance.

There are some key questions at this stage and it is helpful to use a form like the one shown in Table 7.6 which can be attached (together with the lesson observation notes) to the application form of any candidates you feel should not progress through to the final formal interview. This will provide a useful record of a fair and unbiased approach if you are subsequently challenged about the decision. It is not possible to be totally objective when dealing with the human situation of assessing candidates, but you will want to be able to demonstrate that all candidates were judged on the same criteria and that a formal and reasonable process took place.

If you can make this decision before the end of the lunch break, you can then sensitively call out the candidates who are not going through to the formal interview process. You will need to explain briefly your reasons and may offer them a more detailed de-brief if they ring you in a day or two. The notes you have made at the various stages of the process so far will help you to provide clear and constructive feedback to candidates who request it. If travel expenses are applicable, ensure that unsuccessful candidates are given these before they leave the school.

The 'formal' interview

A formal interview normally takes place with governors present and, possibly, one or more LEA representatives. The number of governors present is a matter of choice or governor policy but, generally, the more senior the post the more governors are likely to attend. In appointing a teacher who may be a new entrant to the profession, it is important not to overawe the candidate with a vast array of interviewers. A group made up of two governors, the relevant team leader and a senior leader is likely to be sufficient in most cases.

Involving governors

Governors should be sent copies of the applicants' letters, application forms and references ahead of the interview, as well as a copy of the interview summary sheet to aid initial discussion. They should also be given copies of the job specification and the person specification so that they are clear about the school's requirements for this vacancy.

Room layout

When the interviewing team has assembled and checked that it has got all the necessary papers, thought should be given to the layout of the interview room. All chairs should be the same height and arranged to give all the interviewers a clear sight of the interviewee. A low table with a glass and water jug to hand for the candidate is also desirable, as is a clock placed unobtrusively in the line of sight of the leader of the interview team.

Asking the right questions

A series of interview questions will need to be prepared since all candidates should be asked the same basic questions, although interviewers should be free to probe candidates' individual answers as appropriate. Some interviewers specialise in designing 'master mind' questions that are intricate and challenging and this may be an appropriate approach if you are trying to recruit someone who works well under pressure, can 'think on their feet', and is well up to date with the latest educational issues. The approach offered in Table 7.7 is one in which candidates are given an initial 'soft' question to steady their nerves, and are gradually led through a series of progressively more challenging questions covering both academic and pastoral aspects of being an effective teacher. In designing these questions, it is important to:

- refer back to both the job specification and the person specification. If, for example, you wish to appoint someone who has the self-reflection skills which can enable that person to become a very effective teacher, you will need to design a question which tests these skills;
- identify and list some of the possible desirable answers to your questions (this is particularly helpful when governors or non-specialists are involved

in the interview, and can provide useful evidence if you are later challenged about an appointment);

- design a 'question and answer' sheet based on the above for use in the interview, using a separate sheet to record the responses of each candidate;
- be careful about the number of questions chosen. Nine or ten questions, plus some follow-up questions, will easily take about half an hour and this may be as long as you want to interview each candidate, given that you may be seeing four candidates.

The questions provided in (Table 7.7) are given as examples only of what might be asked in an interview situation when faced with an inexperienced teacher. In practice, schools will want to ask questions that are specific to their own contexts.

The interview team should agree who is to ask each question. Taking questions in turn allows all team members to take notes and to listen carefully. Interviewees should be seen in alphabetical order or some other rational order which is clearly explained to the candidates. Sometimes interviewees are seen in order of how far away they live so that the one with the longest journey home can leave first. As with the start of the day, it is important to explain to candidates what is happening and who they will be seeing. Refreshments should again be available in the waiting area.

It doesn't matter if it is a team leader, senior manager or a governor who is leading the interviewing process at this stage as long as his/her role in the process is clearly signalled to the candidates by taking charge of the start and end of the interview. The team leader should also manage the overall timing of the interview, speeding it up or supplementing questions if the process is going too quickly or lacks pace.

Protocols

At the start of the interview, it is courteous for the interview team leader to:

- stand up to welcome the candidate into the room;
- greet the candidate by name;
- introduce the candidate to governors and others present, making clear what everyone's role is;
- invite the candidate to sit, clearly signalling where s/he should do so, and allowing the candidate time to settle; and
- explain that all candidates will be asked the same questions, that each member of the interview team will ask questions, and that there will be an opportunity for the candidate to ask questions at the end, if s/he has any.

Listening and probing

Once questioning begins, the interview team should focus carefully on what the candidate says in response to the question. Team members should be

Table 7.7 *Possible questions to ask at interview*

Name of candidate:	Name of interviewer:	Date of interview:
Questions	Expected answers and qualities displayed	Interviewer comments
1. Tell me about a good lesson you have taught and why you think it was good? Tell me about a poor lesson you have taught and why you think it was poor.	Good lesson – pace, challenge, clear objectives, variety, matched to pupils' needs, takes account of different learning styles, relates to prior learning or knowledge. Poor lesson – bad start/finish, poor timing, pitched at wrong level, inadequate resources. Look for evidence of thoughtful self reflection, e.g. 'What I learned from this was . . .'	
2. How do you make the teaching of (topic) interesting to pupils of lower ability including those with SEN?	Variety and appropriateness of tasks, lesson 'chunked', pupil involvement, carefully planned literacy activities, use of scaffolding (e.g. writing frames, etc.), clear objectives, strong plenary to reinforce learning, use of rewards/praise. Look for confident knowledge of SEN and how to adapt work for lower ability and SEN classes.	
3. If the class you were teaching in Year X largely had targets of Level Y but were currently operating at Level Z, what would you do?	Knowledge of National Curriculum levels and pupil progress (average progress half a level per year). Knowledge of assessment for learning techniques and their role in pupil progress and independent learning, explicit lesson objectives linked to levels, monitoring, coaching, structuring of work to hit higher levels, impact on lesson planning. Look for evidence of professional commitment to pupil progress.	
4. What is the most difficult topic in your subject to teach to Year X and how would you do it?	Knowledge of subject, and awareness of variety of different teaching techniques to engage the interest of Year X pupils (drama, use of ICT, use of interactive whiteboard, group work, thinking skills, mind maps, etc.).	

(Continued)

Table 7.7 *(Continued)*

Name of candidate:	Name of interviewer:	Date of interview:

Questions	Expected answers and qualities displayed	Interviewer comments
5. As a teacher at this school you are likely to be asked to be a form tutor. What would you do if a member of your form group said she was being bullied by a group of older girls in another class?	Knowledge of some basic approaches to a complaint of bullying: listening to the pupil, speaking to other people who know the pupil well, asking pupil for precise dates and details of alleged bullying and making a record of these, checking when the next situation is likely to be where the pupil feels vulnerable to see how much time there is to take considered action, asking for advice from more senior members of staff or pastoral staff if necessary, reassurance to pupil, setting up 'safe' situation, etc. Look for: awareness of complexities of issues relating to bullying, sensitivity to need for pupil reassurance and safety, judgement and keenness to do something about it but willingness to seek advice if necessary.	
6. What would you do if a pupil in your class refused point-blank to do what you asked him to do?	Knowledge of modern approaches to behaviour management, e.g. assertive discipline, staged sanctions, the language of command. Awareness to operate within the boundaries of the school's behaviour policy. Knowledge that what the teacher says and does is an important influence on pupils. Willingness to repair and move on with relationships with pupils. Importance of keeping class focus on learning not on behaviour of one pupil. Look for confident, assertive approach based on a realistic knowledge of pupil behaviour and teacher expectations.	
7. What part can citizenship play in your teaching of your subject?	Knowledge of cross-curricular themes and the need to incorporate them in subject teaching. Awareness of overall importance of cross-curricular themes.	

Table 7.7 *(Continued)*

Name of candidate:	Name of interviewer:	Date of interview:
Questions	Expected answers and qualities displayed	Interviewer comments
	Look for evidence that the candidate has thought more widely about the curriculum for pupils and has reflected on the implications of this for his/her own teaching.	
8. What personal skills and qualities do you think you could bring to the school if you were appointed to this job?	Look for a confident, self-reflective and realistic response from a candidate who is willing to contribute more than just teaching to the life of the school.	
9. Have you any questions you wish to ask the interviewing panel? (NB: this is not a trick question for candidates but a genuine attempt to ensure that all their questions have been answered in the process they have been through.)	If the selection process has operated well, the candidate should not still have unanswered questions. However, some interviewers use this question to test the preparation and commitment of the candidate.	

encouraged to probe and challenge responses that seem vague or inconsistent. This is the moment when you really want to be convinced that the person in front of you is the strongest candidate to fill the vacancy – and this is your last chance to find out. When it is your turn to ask a question:

- make and maintain strong eye contact with the candidate so that s/he knows instinctively who to focus on without having to keep turning round to include the other interviewers;
- don't worry about not being able to ask questions and write down the candidate's answer – your colleagues are free to write things down at this point;
- give short, non-specific prompts (e.g. *and*? *then what*?), as well as some nods or smiles of encouragement throughout the interview should a candidate lose direction in responding;
- if the candidate rambles or gets totally lost in answering, either help him/her focus using a verbal prompt, referring back to the question asked, or by looking down at a suitable point, breaking eye contact and saying 'thank you' (the latter technique will also help to keep your interviews to time);
- if the candidate lapses into what is obviously a rehearsed or poorly considered reply (e.g. saying 'differentiate' when you ask about work for special needs pupils), be prepared to interrupt to probe the reply: 'Can you tell me exactly what you would do to differentiate *Macbeth*? or 'Give me four examples from your practice in the last few weeks when you have differentiated work and tell me what you did.'

Try to avoid:

- providing the answer to the question if the candidate clearly has no idea what it is;
- making distracting gestures or noises when it is not your turn to ask the question; and
- obviously checking the time when the candidate's response is lengthy or uninteresting.

Drawing the interview to a close

At the end of the interview, the interview team leader should ask the candidate if s/he has any questions for the panel and should establish whether the candidate is still a firm candidate for the post. If the candidate has any uncertainties at this stage, it is better for all concerned that these are aired before an appointment is made. In this situation, you may ask the uncertain candidate to remain until all the other interviews have finished so that you can have a further discussion to try to address his/her concerns. This can also give the candidate a further opportunity for reflection. Normally, you should finish the interview by checking that you have the contact phone number of the individual so that s/he can go home to await the decision of the interviewing panel. Even with only four candidates to consider, it can take an interviewing panel some time to reach a fair judgement and it seems unfair to keep candidates penned in the waiting area waiting while the decision is being made. It can also put pressure on an interview panel to make a hasty decision if they know that candidates are waiting.

Making the decision

In making the decision about which candidate to appoint, you will now need to assemble all the information you have on the candidates and go through it in a systematic manner, taking each candidate in turn. All the individuals who have been involved in the selection process (lesson observers, those involved in professional discussions and those involved in the interview) should now come together.

References

At this stage, you may wish to consider the written references supplied for each candidate. Views are mixed about the usefulness of references because:

- a candidate's right to see his/her own reference makes reference writers understandably bland and cautious;
- reference providers often have mixed motives for providing a positive or negative reference. You can follow up a reference you are uncertain about

by telephoning the reference provider, but this needs to be done before the selection process. The 'it's what's not in it which counts' rule is anecdotally generally held, and you should certainly be suspicious of a reference that does not include the phrase 'good teacher'; and

* some referees will often write lengthy, but formulaic, references.

A systematic approach

You will now want to consider each of the candidates in turn by:

* looking at all aspects of their performance;
* measuring them against your job and person specification;
* considering any additional benefits or qualities they bring to the school; and
* reflecting on how well they might fit into the team where the vacancy exists.

You will need to do this as a group exercise with all those involved in the selection process, using a form similar to the one shown in (Table 7.8). You

Table 7.8   *Grading candidates*

Candidate name:	Grade
Carefully planned and structured teaching	
Lively and imaginative teaching	
Teaching which prompted a good response from pupils	
Good interpersonal skills demonstrated with pupils and colleagues in teaching and throughout selection process	
Thorough and relevant subject and pedagogic knowledge displayed in teaching, professional discussion and interview	
Good written and oral communication skills demonstrated in letter, application, teaching, professional discussion and interview	
Knowledge of pupils' SEN demonstrated in teaching and interview	
An understanding of assessment practice and how it can promote learning demonstrated in interview	
Good judgement, especially in relation to working within school guidelines and knowing when to take advice demonstrated in the interview	
Good behaviour management skills/knowledge demonstrated in lesson observation and interview	
Relevant personal skills: Good judgement especially in relation to working within school guidelines and knowing when to take advice demonstrated in the interview; self reflection demonstrated in the interview; and confidence demonstrated in the interview.	
Additional skills/strengths to bring to the team/wider school	
Qualifications	
Experience of teaching	
Fit with team needs	
Other factors	

Table 7.9 *Scoring candidates and weighting their responses*

Candidate name:	Score	Weighting	Total
Carefully planned and structured teaching		2	
Lively and imaginative teaching		3	
Teaching which prompted a good response from pupils		2	
Good interpersonal skills demonstrated with pupils and colleagues in teaching and throughout selection process		2	
Thorough and relevant subject and pedagogic knowledge displayed in teaching, professional discussion and interview		1	
Good written and oral communication skills demonstrated in letter, application, teaching, professional discussion and interview		1	
Knowledge of pupils' SEN demonstrated in teaching and interview		1	
An understanding of assessment practice and how it can promote learning demonstrated in interview		1	
Good judgement, especially in relation to working within school guidelines and knowing when to take advice demonstrated in the interview		2	
Good behaviour management skills/ knowledge demonstrated is lesson observation and interview		2	
Relevant personal skills: Good judgement especially in relation to working within school guidelines and knowing when to take advice demonstrated in the interview; self reflection demonstrated in the interview; and confidence demonstrated in the interview.		1	
Additional skills/strengths to bring to the team/wider school		1	
Qualifications		1	
Experience of teaching		1	
Fit with team needs		2	
Other factors – specify		1	
		Total	

may wish to grade candidates using the following codes: VS = very strong; S = strong; A = acceptable; W = weak; and VW = very weak. Alternatively, you may choose to grade using 1–5, where 5 = very strong, and 1 = very weak.

On reflection, you may want to weight some factors in this analysis as more important than others. For example, you may feel that matching the person to the needs of the team is more important than the breadth of his/her previous experience. In this case, you will need to score rather than grade the analysis and add a weighting so that some factors have a double or triple score. For example, in the list shown in Table 7.9, 'Lively and imaginative teaching' is valued highly and has a weighting of 3, i.e. 3 × score = total score.

In practice, you are unlikely to have the time to record this level of detail in every interview. However, attempting to sum up candidates in a systematic way in relation to the criteria you set at the beginning of the selection process will help you remain focused on the key task of appointing an effective teacher to fill your particular vacancy.

Case studies: learning through reflection and action

This chapter sets out a series of case studies – based on the reality of school life – that illustrate a variety of authentic scenarios faced by school leaders. In the following case studies we look at some of the stages and situations where a teacher can get 'stuck'. Through 'points for reflection', the reader is invited to consider and propose strategies described in earlier chapters and to call upon his/her own practical knowledge in order to devise plans and actions to support and challenge the teachers portrayed.

Case study 1: Newly Qualified Teacher – Secondary School

Context

Rachel is a young NQT, new to the area and a member of the English Department in a large split-site school of 1,300 pupils. The school is located in a socially disadvantaged area of a town with declining industries, where ethnic groups experience tensions and conflicts in the wider community. These conflicts are regularly 'brought into school'. Rachel's induction to the school amounted to little more than the presentation of the school's 'Handbook of Information' and a brief meeting with her new Head of Department.

> ### Point for reflection
>
> What initial induction practices and support mechanisms should be in place for all new members of staff?
>
> What especial induction support needs to be in place for NQTs?

Concerns

Although Rachel received the statutory reduction in her time-table, attended regular meetings with her Head of Department (also her mentor) and one meeting each half-term with the Deputy Head with responsibility for professional development, she felt generally unsupported. Above all, she felt that there was little in the way of either formal or semi-formal support in school that enabled her to talk to colleagues about any difficulties she was encountering. This situation was compounded because Rachel was located in a mobile classroom, with no permanent staff member next door to her. Established members of staff in the English Department were based in the school's main building.

Rachel felt that the culture in the school made teachers feel defensive about 'admitting' that anything was wrong and therefore reluctant to ask for support when needed. She felt that this attitude was also prevalent in the formal meetings she had with her mentor and the Deputy Head and that she, as a matter of course, had to present a picture that would seem to indicate she was feeling secure and confident.

Point for reflection

What are the factors that help create a positive school/department/area culture?

How can line-managers create supportive meetings and develop an NQT's confidence?

How can line-managers verify the authenticity of the picture an NQT paints of his/her practice?

It was during the course of support the school was receiving from an LEA Literacy Consultant that the concern was raised regarding the behaviour of the pupils in Rachel's classes, and the abuse she was receiving from some of the pupils who were making overt and insulting comments regarding her physical appearance and their views that her lessons were boring.

Point for reflection

At what point should a line-manager become aware of what is happening in an NQT's classroom?

How would the line-manager have learned of this situation?

In the initial meeting with Rachel it quickly became clear that she was very unhappy with the situation and did not know how to start to remedy it. As she saw it, her only focus and solution was to leave the school and apply for a job in a College of Further Education, in the belief that she would not encounter 'behaviour problems' with older students. She described a number of problems she was experiencing:

- Pupils' poor behaviour and attitude towards her.
- Pupils' poor behaviour and attitudes towards each other.
- Pupils' poor attitudes towards learning.
- Her inability to communicate with her Head of Department.
- Her inability to communicate with the Deputy Head responsible for professional development.
- Her feeling of isolation.
- Her lack of awareness about strategies and skills capable of promoting good pupil behaviours for learning.
- Her physical isolation from the rest of the department.
- The school's split-site arrangement presented logistical and practical constraints and obstacles to surmount.

Point for reflection

How can each of these issues be addressed?

Which personnel within the school would you need to hold negotiations with to address the conditions described?

Case study 2: Late entrant NQT – Secondary School

Context

Brian was in his early forties and had entered teaching following a career lecturing in a university, but only on short-term contracts. He was appointed to a large secondary school with 1,200 pupils on roll. The school is considered by the local population to be the best in the area, although the school is by no means in a 'green and leafy part of suburbia'. Brian has good maths subject knowledge, a pleasant manner, and the ability to be reflective and to welcome support to increase his own effectiveness.

Point for reflection

What induction and support programme might the line-manager consider appropriate for an NQT with this background?

He joined a Maths department that suffered from a tired and remote Head of Department. In addition, the Second in the Department was also newly appointed, her teaching experience was in a middle school and she too was struggling to achieve acceptable standards in the classroom. Two other members of the department held roles of responsibility in the Senior Leadership Team and, as a result, were not frequent users of the departmental office, or available to offer an informal support network before school, during breaks, lunchtimes or after school, due to the other demands made on their time. As a consequence, Brian felt isolated within the department, as there was no colleague with whom he felt a sense of camaraderie, or who, he believed, showed any interest in him.

Point for reflection

Given the nature of the staffing in the department, what could be done to offer Brian appropriate support that would be more likely to meet his professional and personal needs?

Concerns

Although Brian's Head of Department was also his mentor, the meetings were infrequent and insubstantial and offered little in terms of backing or practical support. Interestingly, it was the Head of Department who reported to the Assistant Head Teacher (Pastoral) that Brian was having difficulties with his classes.

Brian felt isolated. He was uncertain of the whole-school policies regarding pupil behaviour, codes of dress and the systems for offering rewards and issuing sanctions. He had been left to formulate his own responses to incidents, and attempted to set standards and expectations that he recalled were in place when he was a pupil in school. This would often lead to confrontation with pupils. As a result, Brian was aware that he often might let some behaviour go 'unnoticed', as he did not want to cause further disruption and deal with challenging pupil reactions.

Point for reflection

Whose responsibility is it in your school to ensure that all new members of staff are familiarised with whole-school policies?

Who monitors this and follows things up in a supportive manner?

The obstacles to improving Brian's practice within the classroom proved to be:

- his vocabulary and explanations were too inaccessible for pupils;
- his good subject knowledge was not underpinned with good pedagogy;
- no attempt was made to convey to pupils his expectations of behaviour for learning;
- his responses to and treatment of pupils were inconsistent;
- his failure to carry out sanctions given as 'threats';
- his inability to be able to discuss issues with colleagues in the department;
- his assumption that 'other people' in the school had problems too, and therefore made his difficulties more acceptable.

Point for reflection

As a member of staff with responsibility for the standards in the classroom, how would you seek to address the points above?

Who else in your school needs to be involved in the planning and delivery of effective support for Brian?

If your first lesson observation contained the comments listed below, what would your advice be to Brian?

Observation of Brian's lesson with Year 8

Following an observation of Brian's lesson with a Year 8 mixed–ability class, you note the following:

- The carpet at the entrance to the room curls up and is dangerous – pupils are tripping over it.
- Insufficient number of chairs in the room – seven pupils had to leave the room to obtain a chair from other teachers' rooms causing time delay and disruption to start of lesson.
- No starter activity.

- No Learning Objectives displayed.
- Pupils took a long time to arrive. While waiting, a number of boys who had been early arrivals left the room, apparently without Brian's knowledge.
- Brian distributed scissors and box-shape templates. This was during general noise, chat, banging on desks and calling out. Some pupils began cutting, but no directions had been given. No expectations of whole-class behaviour communicated.
- This resulted in considerable amounts of paper on the floor, some pupils finishing before others had received the equipment, and some misuse of scissors.
- Some pupils 'slipped' into the room at 9.58 a.m. (thirteen minutes late) unnoticed and unchallenged.
- Boy at the front of class continually calling out 'Oy'.
- Boy at back of the class was responding to him. No intervention from Brian.
- The class was asked a number of times to quieten down and to 'shush'.
- An explanation of cubes was given over considerable class noise and chatter – some of which was to do with the maths, but much wasn't. Brian did ask for 'hush', and the majority of pupils complied. Those that didn't continued to talk over Brian's teaching.
- Boy with the mess on the floor told he would stay behind at break. Did not happen.
- Boy went out of the room, returned with wet paper towel. Towel thrown at another pupil.
- Worksheet distributed, but again considerable noise level.
- Two thirds of the class were on task. One third were overt in their off-task behaviours. The high noise levels required Brian to explain again to individuals. During this time, two pupils started throwing the cubes at various people in the class – seemingly unnoticed and unchallenged.
- Boy who had been sent outside started to create a disturbance with pupils at the back by opening the door, calling in and throwing card back and forth with boy on back row.
- Cubes were taken off two boys.
- One of the boys started to then take cubes off other pupils.
- Boy who was sent out carried on opening the door and causing a disruption.
- Another pupil shredded his worksheet with the scissors.
- Pupil threw another cube at girl's head. No intervention.
- The two boys then got out of their seats, went to the teacher's desk and took a handful of cubes out of the bag – unnoticed.
- Same pupils had done no work and said they didn't know what to do.
- Boy who was outside of the class stayed there for the rest of the lesson.
- Some pupils began to pack up before the bell had gone and before any instruction had been given by the teacher. When the bell sounded pupils left the room without any formal dismissal routine.

Point for reflection

What targets would you focus on with Brian?

What timescale would you use?

What level of monitoring and support would you feel is appropriate?

Case study 3: Late entrant NQT – Primary School

Context

Nick, aged 25, was appointed to an inner city primary school of 360 pupils, having left a career running his own shop. It soon became apparent to the Head Teacher that he was experiencing considerable difficulties in teaching his Year 4 class. Not only were other members of staff aware of the level of noise and disruption, but the school has also received letters of complaint from some parents regarding Nick's teaching methods.

Point for reflection

How does your school respond in the event of complaints from parents about under-performing teachers?

Concerns

The school processes for the monitoring of the quality of lesson planning and the regular tracking of each individual pupil's progress soon highlighted the conflicting elements of Nick's approach. He seemed genuinely happy teaching, and loved the company of the children. His planning was superb, but he was unable to put it into practice. Furthermore, Nick was unable to see what difficulties the children were experiencing. He held the opinion that because his planning was thorough there wasn't anything else on which he could improve.

To enable him to gain more insight into what makes an effective teacher, his lessons were covered and Nick was then able to observe the good practice of other colleagues who were able to demonstrate a range of styles, strategies and skills in the classroom. An action plan was then devised by the Head Teacher that served to formalise the package of support Nick was to receive, together with the school's expectations of him. The Head Teacher showed a respect for his views and took them into account. Nick was given the opportunity to suggest some of his own action points and the resulting training needs were identified, resourced, and timescales attached to them. It was only at this stage that Nick began to understand the seriousness of his position. The monitoring would continue, as it did for all staff, and a review of Nick's progress was set for the next half-term.

Nick had additional classroom support. The school enlisted the support of the LEA to work with Nick and to monitor and confirm the judgements the school made. Despite the rigour of the school's support and the Head Teacher's desire to see Nick become a reflective and effective teacher, after the third term he made the decision to leave teaching young pupils and to enter a career in teaching ICT to adults.

He is now a successful educator in this area, and is appreciative of the efforts the primary school made on his behalf. As he sees it, 'If the school hadn't taken the time and interest, I would have carried on never knowing that I wasn't really suited.'

Point for reflection

Should it always be possible to predict how well suited someone is to the profession?

Are there any other less formal strategies that the school could have used that you feel Nick might have responded well to?

Case study 4: Mature teacher returning to teaching – Middle School

Context

For two years, Caroline has been teaching French in a rural middle school of 300 pupils and 13 full-time staff, having been made redundant from her previous school. This Church of England middle school has historically enjoyed the benefits of being in a catchment area that mainly serves a higher socio-economic population. Until recently, the school had not considered itself as suffering from any poor pupil behaviour and needing to have contact with parents who are unsupportive or with poor parenting skills. It is the lack of expertise in this respect that exacerbates the position that Caroline finds herself in.

> ## Point for reflection
>
> What can the school do to help itself in this position?
>
> Who in the school needs to be involved?
>
> What other outside agencies would the school find it beneficial to liaise with?

Concerns

Caroline is employed on a part-time contract, which suits her needs well. She has two children of her own that she uses as reference points as to why the problems she experiences with some classes are 'the pupils' fault' and not anything to do with her own teaching and management skills. However, she does rely heavily on the presence of her allotted TA to obtain and sustain a level of orderly pupil behaviour that will enable Caroline to teach the planned lesson. Caroline does use the school 'incident referral slip' mechanism to report to Senior Management. It is the combination of the number of slips received and the TA's views that were subsequently sought that informed the school of the nature of the problem.

> ## Point for reflection
>
> What systems could the school utilise to address concerns regarding a teacher's effectiveness before the situation deteriorates too far?
> At what point would the line-manager become knowledgeable about the issues a teacher is experiencing?
> How can a school develop a strong culture of looking at the pedagogy of teaching and embedding the principles that lie within it?

Caroline perceives that the following are adversely affecting her ability to establish and sustain good relationships and good learning patterns in her pupils:

- Other teachers find some classes difficult too.
- Sometimes the TA is not able to be in the class.
- The school's senior management is weak.
- Pupils are able to do as they want.
- There is inadequate support from within the school for those pupils with particular identified needs, both behaviourally and educationally.
- She is unable to administer sanctions as the systems are too cumbersome.
- She finds the school's rewards system ineffective as pupils feel negatively about it.

> **Point for reflection**
>
> If Caroline was on the staff of your school, how would you help her
> to address what she sees as the issues (above) that are entirely
> rooted in school systems and the performance of others?

Observation of Caroline's lesson with Year 6

Following an observation of Caroline's lesson with Year 6, you note the
following:

- There is a five-minute space between lessons to allow for pupil movement,
  but a high percentage of pupils arrived very late, and noisily.
- Caroline began to talk over pupil chat, and then gave the instruction to be
  quiet.
- No learning objectives for the lesson displayed or referred to.
- Recap of yesterday's lesson, rewards and stickers referred to. (These were
  not actually given out at any point during the lesson.)
- Caroline expressed clear rule about bags not being brought into class.
  Pupils complied by removing them.
- Girl was asked to put a reading book away, didn't, no acknowledgement –
  girl offered non-verbal challenge. Her behaviour deteriorated from that
  point onwards. She then became louder, got out of her chair, called out,
  displaying openly defiant behaviour.
- Other overt behaviours from a group of boys revolved around playing on
  the top of their desks with toy cars and snatching them from one another.
  No acknowledgement or intervention from Caroline.
- Caroline then asked girl with book to put it away for a second time. Girl
  failed to comply with the request.
- Caroline then took the cars from the boys.
- The boys picked up on the girl who had been asked again to put her book
  away, and hadn't, but they had had the cars taken from them. The boys
  became cantankerous.
- Class behaviour began to deteriorate as more pupils became argumenta-
  tive, refusing to participate, tardy in starting written task.
- Caroline made reference to a boy having an incident slip (none was issued
  at any point during or after the lesson).
- Boy sent outside the room for interfering with another pupil who was
  working. He did not return.
- Praise was given to individual pupils who were getting on with their work.
- Another boy was sent out having indulged in extremely loud attention-
  seeking negative behaviour.
- Reference was made to the whole class about the possibility of staying in at
  lunchtime. This was not actually issued, despite continuing poor behaviour.

- No plenary.
- Dismissal was expressed in French. Pupils were relatively orderly.

Point for reflection

What approach could the line-manager take in order to be helpful to Caroline, bearing in mind she considers herself to be an experienced teacher?

What aspects of this lesson observation would you consider to be the most pertinent features preventing Caroline from teaching effectively?

Case study 5: Mature teacher returning to teaching – Primary School

Context

Yvonne returned to teaching after a break of seven years in which she raised her family. She was appointed to a very small village primary school with 75 pupils on roll. The very size of the school, the small number of staff, and the nature of the close-knit community meant that word soon spread that all was not well in Yvonne's class.

Point for reflection

Does the size and complexity of the school have a bearing on the under-performance of teachers and any strategies put in place for dealing with it?

Concerns

Yvonne was regarded as a delightful person by all who knew her – adults and pupils alike – but despite this, she had very real problems in gaining and maintaining a class discipline necessary to pupils' successful learning. Yvonne found it difficult to accept that there really was a problem. The Head Teacher felt that Yvonne was over-prepared which caused her to become too inflexible. Her lack of confidence following a break from teaching seemed to be a prime cause of the rigidity in her approach. Despite being monitored in the classroom, Yvonne still experienced difficulties in controlling the class. She continued to plan the lessons well, but was still unable to improve their delivery.

Halfway through this process Yvonne went to her professional association. Consequently the Head Teacher consulted with the LEA who monitored her teaching and set an action plan in place. Yvonne was given appropriate support, training and the opportunity to improve, but still there was no improvement. Yvonne continued to deny that there was a problem. At this point, formal capability proceedings were put in place. Yvonne left the school before the designated period of time had elapsed.

Point for reflection

How would you attempt to deal with Yvonne's reluctance to accept that there is a problem with her practice?

Should the support of a teacher's identified needs, written into an action plan, resourced and carried out, always be expected to be effective?

Case study 6: Mature member of staff – Secondary School

Context

Dennis is a Science teacher in a small secondary school with 550 pupils on role. He is very close to retirement age, but continues to teach in order to meet his financial commitments. The school is performing poorly in both Key Stage 3 and Key Stage 4 and has a dwindling sixth form.

Point for reflection

What opportunities are there in the whole-school situation of under-performance?

How might these opportunities be presented to all staff?

What processes and deployment of staff are necessary to ensure that progress is being secured?

The Head of Department is new and has a good grasp of what needs to be done in the department and whole school in order to secure improvements. He is an associate member of the Senior Leadership Team (SLT).

Point for reflection

How might the Head of Department's Senior Leadership role assist him in focusing on Dennis's teaching skills and beliefs about pupils?

Concerns

Dennis has been a teacher for his entire career and is a well-liked member of staff. He is perceived to be 'good old Dennis'. He believes that it is a sign of the times that his classes are unruly and that the pupil performance data indicates serious under-performance. He feels that only one person on the SLT is effective, and sees the lack of drive and initiative in the others as excusing his own ineffectiveness as a teacher.

The Head of Department does not want to antagonise Dennis, and does not want to encourage a backlash from other members of staff who are supportive of Dennis. For this reason the drive towards departmental improvements have tended to be generic and not aimed specifically at any one individual. This has failed to secure the improvement that the Head of Department hoped to see in Dennis.

Point for reflection

What tone is likely to be the most productive approach for the Head of Department to take in the first meeting with Dennis designed to address some of the issues?

In discussing school improvement issues with Dennis, he made it clear that the obstacles to improvement in his classes are:

- Poor literacy and general knowledge levels of pupils.
- Boys not being motivated, while the girls work hard.
- His tendency not to discipline pupils.
- Having a top set after teaching low sets.
- Lack of non-contact time in one of the two-week time-tables.

- Not being able to give classes work to do while he does something else.
- He doesn't find satisfaction in the few pupils who do 'see the light'.
- Pupils are happy to sit and copy.
- Pupils don't take any notice of marking in exercise books so he doesn't put red pen on the books, but does read to see the work that is done.

Point for reflection

How can the Head of Department respond constructively to Dennis's firmly held beliefs?

Who else in the school might assist the Head of Department to support Dennis?

Observation of Dennis's lesson with Year 10

Following an observation of Dennis's lesson with Year 10, you note the following:

- Pupils were asked to put coats on the side bench. They did so, somewhat tardily, possibly indicating this is not a routine that happens automatically.
- Dennis attempted to take the register over pupil noise and while some were still entering. Some boys pushing each other.
- 'Right, shut up, listen' was the first opening address to the whole class.
- The whiteboards were fully prepared for the lesson.
- Little and poor quality of room display.
- No learning objectives displayed or referred to.
- Dennis began the explanation building from last week's lesson, but allowed some pupils to talk continuously. Some pupils were named, but this was ineffective, and this was not acknowledged.
- Dennis said boy's name three times then said boy would have to be taken out. Boy questioned why he had to go out when others were also misbehaving. This then led to argument between the two.
- The girls on the back row appeared far more compliant as they were quieter than the boys, yet they were unfocused on the explanation and were involved in diversions such as doodling and fidgeting. This was unchallenged.
- Girl's name was called. She responded with an insolent tone 'What?' No response from Dennis.
- Another boy was told he would go on a discipline sheet.
- Another boy was told to go out, he argued, Dennis did not insist.
- Both boys and girls showed no regard for listening to the teacher, behaviours were both overt and covert.

- During the practical drawing part of the lesson, rulers were used as weapons by boys. No intervention from Dennis. Not noticed or heard?
- Dennis busy going round to pupils explaining individually what they should be doing.
- Boy was asked to hand over the ruler. He did so begrudgingly, and was then sent out of the room.
- While Dennis still encouraging individuals to work, other pupils are unsupervised and literally doing nothing.
- Whole-class instruction 'Right settle down' met with general disregard. Some individual names were called, then a whole-class 'Shut up'. Dennis continued with individual names but these were still disregarded. His voice got louder and he showed the habit of repeatedly telling the class to 'Shut up'.
- A pencil case was thrown. Was seen and acknowledged.
- Class was asked to copy what was on the board into their exercise books.
- Some pupils were singing, but only one boy was picked on when others were also doing it.
- Dennis then went round each pupil asking them their Newton weight. This revealed how many had not done the work or understood what to do, and was very demanding of Dennis's attention.
- Drawing the lesson together at the end was done through considerable pupil noise. Threats of names being taken and pupils being kept at the end of assembly tomorrow issued.
- Some boys were throwing paper planes.
- Books were collected, but no checking of whether the work had been done.
- Pupils were asked to sit down, a number were standing, but again one boy was singled out and asked to sit.
- Chocolates were given to pupils dependent on the answers to quiz in last lesson.
- Pupil noise level loud throughout.
- The class were told 'off you go' but no orderly exit established.

Point for reflection

As the observer of these teacher/pupil interactions, what strategies would you recommend Dennis to employ?

What are the two key areas for Dennis to focus on?

What might work as an incentive for Dennis to enable him to view the support process positively?

Bibliography

Armstrong, M. (2000) *Performance Management*. London: Kogan Page.

Bates, R. A. and Holton, E. F. (1995) 'Computerised performance monitoring: a review of human resources issues', *Human Resource Management Reviews,* Winter, pp. 267–88.

Bernadin, H. K., Kane, J. S., Ross, S., Spina, J. D. and Johnson, D. L. (1995) 'Performance appraisal design, development and implementation', in G. R. Ferris, S. D. Rosen and D. J. Barnum (eds), *Handbook of Human Resource Management*. Cambridge, MA: Blackwell.

Bloud, D., Keogh, R. and Walker, D. (eds) (1985) *Reflection: Turning Experience into Learning*. London: Kogan Page.

Brumbach, G. B. (1988) 'Some ideas, issues and predictions about performance management', *Public Personnel Management,* Winter, pp. 387–402.

Canter, L. and Canter, M. (1992) *Assertive Discipline: Positive Behavior Management for Today's Classroom*. California: Canter & Associates, Inc.

Dean, J. (2002) *Implementing Performance Management: A Handbook for Schools*. London: Routledge Falmer.

DfEE (Department for Education and Employment) (2000) *Performance Management in Schools: Performance Management Framework* (DfEE 0051/2000). London: The Stationery Office.

DfES (Department for Education and Skills) (2001) *Learning and Teaching: A Strategy for Professional Development*. London: The Stationery Office.

DfES (Department for Education and Skills) (2005) *Learning Behaviour: The Report of the Practitioners' Group on School Behaviour and Discipline*. London: The Stationery Office.

Fidler, B. and Atton, T. (1999) *Poorly Performing Staff in Schools and How to Manage Them*. London: Routledge.

Fullan, M. and Hargreaves, D. (1992) *What's Worth Fighting for in Your School? Working Together for Improvement*. Toronto: Ontario Public School Teachers' Federation; New York: Teachers College Press; Buckingham: Open University Press.

Ginott, H. (1972) *Teacher and Child*. New York: Macmillan.

Griffin, J. and Tyrell, I. (2003) *Human Givens: A New Approach to Emotional Health and Clear Thinking*. Chalvington: HG Publishing.

Hay/McBer (2000) *Research into Teacher Effectiveness: A Model of Teacher Effectiveness*. Report to the DfEE. Available at: http://www.dfee.gov.uk.

Hogg, M. and Vaughan, G. (2005) *Social Psychology* (4th Edition). Harlow: Pearson Education.

Honey, P. and Mumford, A. (1988) *Manual of Learning Styles*. Maidenhead: Peter Honey.

Industry in Education (2000) *Milestone or Millstone? Performance Management in Schools-Reflections on the Experiences of Industry*. Radlett: Industry in Education.

James, C. and Connolly, U. (2000) *Effective Change in Schools,* London: Routledge Falmer.

Jones, J. L. (2001) *Performance Management for School Improvement*. London: David Fulton Publishers.

Jones, J. L. (2005) *Management Skills in Schools: A Resource for School Leaders*. London: Paul Chapman Publishing.

Kane, J. S. (1996) 'The conceptualisation and representation of total performance effectiveness', *Human Resource Management Review,* Summer, pp. 123–45.

Louden, W. (1991) *Understanding Teaching: Continuity and Change in Teachers' Knowledge*. London: Cassell.

MacBeath, J. (1999) *Schools Must Speak For Themselves: The Case for School Self-evaluation*. London: Routledge.

McKenzie, J. (2001) *Perform or Else: From Discipline to Performance*. London: Routledge.

McKernan, J. (1999) *Curriculum Action Research* (2nd Edition). London: Kogan Page.

Megginson, D. and Boydell, T. (1979) *A Manager's Guide to Coaching*. London: BACIE.

Muijs, D. and Reynolds, D. (2005) *Effective Teaching: Evidence and Practice*. London: Paul Chapman Publishing.

OECD (Organization for Economic Co-operation and Development) (2005) *Teachers Matter: Attracting, Developing and Retaining Effective Teachers*. London: OECD Publishing.

Ofsted (Office for Standards in Education) (2003a) *Handbook for Inspecting Primary and Nursery Schools*. London: Ofsted.

Ofsted (Office for Standards in Education) (2003b) *Handbook for Inspecting Secondary Schools*. London: Ofsted.

Ofsted (Office for Standards in Education) (2003c) *Framework 2003 – Inspecting Schools*. London: Ofsted.

Ofsted (Office for Standards in Education) (2004) *Annual Report of Her Majesty's Chief Inspector of Schools: Standards and Quality isn Education 2002/03*. London: Ofsted.

Parry, G. (1991) 'Teacher incompetence and the courts: the American experience', *Education and the Law*, 3(2), pp. 71–8.

Pease, A. (1990) *Body Language: How to Read Others' Thoughts by Their Gestures*. London: Sheldon Press.

Rhodes, C. and Beneicke, S. (2003) 'Professional development support for poorly performing teachers: challenges and opportunities for school managers in addressing teacher learning needs', *Journal of In-Service Education*, 29(1), pp. 121–38.

Robertson, J. (2002) 'The boss, the manager and the leader approaches to dealing with disruption' in W. A. Rogers (ed.), *Teacher Leadership and Behaviour Management*. London: Paul Chapman Publishing.

Rogers, B. (2003) *Cracking the Hard Class*. London: Paul Chapman Publishing.

Rogers, W. A. (ed.) (2002) *Teacher Leadership and Behaviour Management*. London: Paul Chapman Publishing.

Rogers, W. A. (2003) *Classroom Behaviour*. London: Paul Chapman Publishing.

Ross, D. D. (1990) 'Programmatic Structures for the Preparation of Reflective Teachers' in R. T. Clift, R. W. Houston, and M. C. Pugach, (eds), *Encouraging Reflective Practice in Education: An Analysis of Issues and Programs*. New York: Teachers College, Columbia University.

Schaffer, R. H. (1991) 'Demand better results and get them', *Harvard Business Review*, March–April, pp.142–9.

Stoll, L. and Myers, K. (1998) *No Quick Fixes: Perspectives on Schools in Difficulty*. London: Falmer Press.

Vass, A. (2002) 'Teaching that works: using the human givens in the classroom', *Human Givens*, 9(3), pp. 37–43.

Weightman, J. (1999) *Managing People*. London: Institute of Personnel and Development/ Cromwell Press.

Wragg, E. C. (1999) *An Introduction to Classroom Observation*. Routledge: London.

Wragg, E. C., Haynes, G. S., Wragg, C. M. and Chamberlain, R. P. (2000) *Failing Teachers?* London: Routledge.

Index

Added to the page number 'f' denotes a figure and 't' denotes a table.

A

accountability vii
  growth in viii
  personal practice and 109–10
active listening, demonstrating 88–9
activists
  coach learning styles 88t
  coachee learning styles 87t
advertisements for posts 118–19
annual training plans for Professional
    Development Groups (PDGs)
    101–2, 103t
applicants
  details sent to 119, 120t, 122–4
  organising responses from 125
  records of contact with 125f
  short-listing *see* short-listing applicants
  testing for desirable attributes in
    120, 121t
assertive statements 65
assertive teachers, body language 60

B

behaviour management issues 39t
behaviour management
    techniques 63–6
  general principles 65–6
behaviour of teachers *see* teacher behaviour
beliefs, underlying 111–13
blocking 65
body language
  of teaching styles 58–60
  to demonstrate active listening 88–9
  using influential 57–8
brainstorming 105
'broken record' technique 62–3

C

case studies
  learning through reflection and action 144–58
  late entrant newly qualified teacher
    (NQT) - primary school 150–1
  late entrant newly qualified teacher
    (NQT) – secondary school 146–50
  mature member of staff – secondary
    school 155–8
  mature teacher returning to teaching –
    middle school 151–4
  mature teacher returning to teaching –
    primary school 154–5
  newly qualified teacher (NQT) –
    secondary school 144–6
  for the reflective awareness model 49–52
  use in group training 110–11
causes of under-performance 7, 8t, 25f
choice and consequence 65
choice direction 64, 65
closed questions 92t
coaching 83–8
  knowledge, skills and behaviours required
    84, 85t
  STAR model for gauging success 95
  styles and skills 84–7
coaching relationship, learning styles
    and 87–8
competency/capability proceedings 44
confrontation, avoiding 6, 93
conscious competence 48
'conscious competence' learning
    matrix 47–9
conscious incompetence 47–8
consequence, choice and 65
constructive criticism, strategies for
    giving 91, 93

CPD (continuous professional
    development) 98–115
  elements 81–2
  and Professional Development Groups
      (PDGs) *see* Professional Development
      Groups (PDGs)
  and Professional Development Portfolios 104
  provision of opportunities for 81–2
'culture of blame' 16
curriculum and planning issues 39t

D

description of reality 65
directions
  choice 64, 65
  pause 63
  simple 65
  'when … then' 63
directive coaching 84
directive feedback 94–5
distraction and diversion 63

E

effective teachers 4–5
  body language 57
  pupils' perceptions of 54
elicitive coaching 84
elicitive feedback 94
examination results, analysis of 27–8
exclusion of pupils 65
exit procedure 65
expectations, conveying 69–71

F

feedback 91–5
  strategies for constructive 91, 93
  styles 94–5
  see also question and feedback
'first cut' in the selection process 133–4
focused discussion in group training 105
focused listening 85
formal identification of the need for support 27–8
'formal' interviews 135–40
  drawing to a close 140
  involving governors 135
  listening and probing 136, 139–40
  protocols 136
  questions for 135–6, 137t–9t
  room layout 135
furniture, layout of 72

G

'glazed look' listening 90
group training, planning for 105–15

H

hostile teachers, body language 59–60

I

'I' statements, using 63
individual difficulties and ineffective teaching
    16, 18–22
individual plans, agreeing 78–9, 80t
induction 98–9
ineffective teachers 17t
ineffective teaching 15–25
  and the immediate working context 22
  and individual difficulties 16, 18–22
  and the wider school context 22–4
influential speech, using 62–6
informal identification of the need for support 29
interaction zones 61
interventions *see* behaviour management techniques
interviews, 'formal' *see* 'formal' interviews
intimate zone 61

J

job descriptions 121–2, 123f–4f

L

language *see* speech
layout of rooms 72
  for 'formal' interviews 135
leading questions 92t
learned responses, application of 63–6
learning styles, and the coaching relationship 87–8
Learning and Teaching: A Strategy for Professional
    Development 81
lesson observation
  as part of the selection process 131–2
  of under-performing teachers 35–40
    follow-up discussions 37
    setting targets after 37–40
    training for 35–7
lesson planning 68–9
  proforma for 70t
letters of application 124–5
listening
  effective skills for 88–90
    barriers to 90
  as a skill in coaching 85
Local Management of Schools (LMS) vii

M

'matter over mind' listening 90
mature teachers, case studies 151–8
middle leaders, induction for 98
middle schools, case study of mature teacher
    returning to teaching 151–4

Milestone or Millstone? Performance Management in Schools: Reflections on the Experiences of Industry 10
monitoring, and the performance management cycle 79
multiple questions 92t

N

newly qualified teachers (NQTs)
    case studies
        primary schools 150–1
        secondary schools 144–50
    induction for 98
non-directive coaching 84
non-verbal messages 64
nursery schools
    Ofsted's summary of poor teaching/learning 14t
    Ofsted's summary of unsatisfactory teaching/learning 13t

O

observation schedules 36t
observing lessons *see* lesson observation
'obviously' listening 90
Ofsted inspections viii
    criteria 12–15
on-off listening 90
'open ears-closed mind' listening 90
open questions 92t

P

partial agreement 63
passive teachers 39
    body language 58–9
pause direction 63
performance
    definition 3–4
    see also under-performance
Performance and Assessment Data Analysis (PANDA) reports 27
performance management viii
    benefits 10
    and building trust 88, 89t
    coaching as an element *see* coaching
    concept 75–6
    preconditions 76t
    and tackling under-performance 9–10
performance management cycle 76–81
    monitoring 79
    planning 77–9
    review 79–81
performance reviews 75–97
    and giving feedback *see* feedback
    in the performance management cycle 79–81

performance reviews *cont.*
    and provision of professional development 81–2
    and questioning techniques 90–1, 92t
person specifications 119, 120t, 121, 122t
personal practice and accountability 109–10
personal zone 61
physical environment 72–4
    layout of furniture 72
    repair and renovation 73
    wall displays 72–3
physical proximity 63
planned ignoring 64
planning 67–71
    and the performance management cycle 77–9
    see also support plans
planning issues, curriculum and 39t
policies on teaching vii
'poor performers' 4, 15
positive, being 66–7
positive repetition 64
posts
    advertising for 118–19
    defining 119–20
    job descriptions for 121–2, 123f-4f
    person specifications for 119, 120t, 121, 122t
    see also vacancies
pragmatists
    coach learning styles 88t
    coachee learning styles 87t
praise
    using 66–7
    see also proximity praise
primary schools
    case studies
        late entrant newly qualified teacher (NQT) 150–1
        mature teacher returning to teaching 154–5
    Ofsted's summary of poor teaching/learning 14t
    Ofsted's summary of unsatisfactory teaching/learning 13t
    Professional Development Groups (PDGs) in 99
    under-performance 11
privately understood signals 63
probing questions 92t
professional development *see* CPD (continuous professional development)
Professional Development Groups (PDGs) 99–104
    annual training plans 101–2, 103t
    chairing 100–1
    composition 100
    and continuing professional development needs

Professional Development Groups (PDGs) *cont.*
  identification of 101, 102t
  responding to 101–2, 103t
functions 99–100
  and planning activities 102–3, 104t
    for group training 105–15
  purpose 99
Professional Development Portfolios 104
professional relationships between staff and
    pupils 18–21
  importance of 54
professional standards for teachers 12
proximity praise 63
public zone 61
pupils
  behaviour 53–4
  creating professional relationships with 18–21
  exclusion 65
  perceptions of teacher behaviour 54–6
  re-establishing working relationships with 64

Q

question and feedback 63, 65
questioning techniques 90–1, 92t

R

reality, description of 65
records of contact with applicants 125f
recruitment and selection 116–43
  advertising 118–19
  being systematic 116–17
  defining posts 119–20
  details sent to applicants 119, 120t, 122–4
  job descriptions 121–2, 123f–4f
  letters of application 124–5
  making the decision 140
    systematic approach to 141–3
    use of references 140–1
  organising responses from applicants 125
  selection process *see* selection process
  short-listing applicants *see* short-listing applicants
  timing 117–18
'red-flag' listening 90
references, use in recruitment and selection 140–1
reflection
  case studies *see* case studies, learning through
    reflection and action
  definition 45
  questions to assist 52–3, 68
  see also self-reflection
reflective awareness model 47–52
  case studies for 49–52
reflective consciousness 49
reflective questions 92t
reflective teachers 45–7

reflectors
  coach learning styles 88t
  coachee learning styles 87t
reform of teaching vii
relationships *see* coaching relationship;
    professional relationships;
    working relationships
repetition, using positive 64
review, and the performance management
    cycle 79–81
rewards, use of 66–7
role play in group training 105
role of teachers 1–2
rule reminders 64, 65
'the rule of three' 63

S

scenario writing, for group training 110–11
schools
  consequences of under-performance 1–3
  effect of context on ineffective teaching 22–4
  tours of 132
  see also middle schools; nursery schools;
    primary schools
secondary schools
  case studies
    mature member of staff 155–8
    newly qualified teachers (NQTs) 144–50
  Ofsted's summary of poor
    teaching/learning 14t
  Ofsted's summary of unsatisfactory
    teaching/learning 13t
  under-performance 11
selection process 129–40
  creating the right impression for
    candidates 130–1
  and encouraging discussion 132–3
  'formal' interviews *see* 'formal' interviews
  invitations to short-listed candidates
    to attend interview 130
  lesson observation 131–2
  lunch and the 'first-cut' 133–4
  time-tables for 129–30
  tours of schools 132
self-identification of the need for support 26–7
self-reflection 45–74
  lack of 26–7
  using 52–74
  see also reflection
short-listing applicants 125–9
  how many to short-list 129
  initial analysis 126–7
  invitations to attend interview 130
  summarising key facts about applicants
    127, 128t

simple direction 65
sinking teachers 17t
social zone 61
speech, using influential 62–6
staff
    professional relationships between
        pupils and 18–21
    see also teachers
Staff Development for School
    Improvement Plans 102–3, 104t
STAR model for gauging coaching success 95
struggling teachers 17t
'stuck record' technique 65
stuck teachers 17t
support 26–44
    failure of 44
    identifying the need for 26–9
        formal identification 27–8
        informal identification 29
        self-identification 26–7
    process *see* teacher support process
    providers 29–31
support plans 40–3

T

tactical ignoring 63, 64
take up time 64
teacher behaviour
    being positive 66–7
    the body language of teaching styles 58–60
    and interaction zones 61
    pupils' perceptions 54–6
    using influential body language 57–8
    using influential speech 62–6
teacher effectiveness *see* effective teachers
teacher support process 31–43
    failure of 44
    initial discussion 32–3
        difficulties with 33–4
    initial lesson observation 35–40
        follow-up discussions 37
        setting targets after 37–40
        training for 35–7
    review meetings 43
    support plans 40–3
teachers
    differentiated terms for under-performing 17t
    meeting the development needs of 98–9
    professional standards for 12
    role 1–2
    see also assertive teachers; effective teachers;
        hostile teachers; mature teachers; newly
        qualified teachers (NQTs); passive
        teachers; reflective teachers

Teachers Matter: Attracting, Developing and
    Retaining Effective Teachers viii
teaching
    ineffective *see* ineffective teaching
    policy vii
    reform of vii
teaching styles, body language of 58–60
team analysis matrices 120t
team leaders, coaching skills for 83–8
test results, analysis of 27–8
theorists
    coach learning styles 88t
    coachee learning styles 87t
training 102t
    leading to ineffective teaching 21–2
    for lesson observation 35–7
    see also CPD (continuous professional
        development); group training
trust, building 88, 89t

U

unconscious competence 48f, 49
unconscious incompetence 47, 48f
under-performance vii–viii, 1–10
    avoiding direct conflict and dispensing
        criticism 6, 93
    causes 7, 8t, 25f
    consequences for schools 1–3
    constituents 11–15
    definition 3–4
    early indications 46
    recognition of 5–7, 11–25
    taking responsibility for dealing with 7
    using performance management to
        tackle 9–10
under-performing teachers 16, 17t
underlying beliefs, examination of 111–13

V

vacancies 117
    see also posts
visualising 105

W

wall displays 72–3
'when...then' directions 63
working context, and ineffective teaching 22
working relationships with pupils,
    re-establishing 64

Z

'zero tolerance of failure' 16